The Wadsworth Themes in American Literature Series

1945–PRESENT

THEME 17

Race and Ethnicity in the Melting Pot

Henry Hart
College of William and Mary

Jay Parini
Middlebury College
General Editor

D0024332

WADSWORTH
CENGAGE Learning

Australia • Brazil • Japan • Korea • Mexico • Singapore • Spain • United Kingdom • United States

WADSWORTH
CENGAGE Learning

**The Wadsworth Themes in American
   Literature Series, 1910–1945**
**Theme 17: Race and Ethnicity in the
   Melting Pot**
Henry Hart, Jay Parini

Publisher, Humanities: *Michael Rosenberg*

Senior Development Editor: *Michell Phifer*

Assistant Editor: *Megan Garvey*

Editorial Assistant: *Rebekah Matthews*

Associate Development Project Manager:
   Emily A. Ryan

Executive Marketing Manager: *Mandee
   Eckersley*

Senior Marketing Communications Manager:
   Stacey Purviance

Senior Project Manager, Editorial Production: *Lianne Ames*

Senior Art Director: *Cate Rickard Barr*

Senior Print Buyer: *Mary Beth Hennebury*

Permissions Editor: *Margaret Chamberlain-
   Gaston*

Permissions Researcher: *Writers Research
   Group, LLC*

Production Service: *Kathy Smith*

Text Designer: *Frances Baca*

Photo Manager: *Sheri Blaney*

Photo Researcher: *Sharon Donahue*

Cover Designer: *Frances Baca*

Cover Image: *© age fotostock/Superstock*

Compositor: *Graphic World, Inc.*

For product information and technology assistance, contact us at
Cengage Learning Academic Resource Center, 1-800-423-0563
For permission to use material from this text or product,
submit all requests online at **www.cengage.com/permissions.**
Further permissions questions can be e-mailed to
permissionrequest@cengage.com.

Library of Congress Control Number: 2008925325

ISBN-13: 978-1-4282-6249-2

ISBN-10: 1-4282-6249-0

Wadsworth Cengage Learning
25 Thomson Place
Boston, 02210
USA

Cengage Learning products are represented in Canada by Nelson Education, Ltd.

For your course and learning solutions, visit
academic.cengage.com.

Purchase any of our products at your local college store
or at our preferred online store **www.ichapters.com.**

The credits on page 94 constitute an extension of the copyright page.

Printed in the United States of America
1 2 3 4 5 6 7 12 11 10 09 08

Contents

Preface

WHAT IS AMERICA? HOW HAVE WE DEFINED OURSELVES over the past five centuries, and dealt with the conflict of cultures, the clash of nations, races, ethnicities, religious visions, and class interests? How have we thought about ourselves, as men and women, in terms of class and gender? How have we managed to process a range of complex and compelling issues?

The Wadsworth Themes in American Literature Series addresses these questions in a sequence of 21 booklets designed especially for classroom use in a broad range of courses. There is nothing else like them on the market. Each booklet has been carefully edited to frame issues of importance, with attention to the development of key themes. Teachers and students have consistently found these mini-anthologies immensely productive in the classroom, as the texts we have chosen are provocative, interesting to read, and central to the era under discussion. Each thematic booklet begins with a short essay that provides the necessary historical and literary context to address the issues raised in that theme. In addition, many of the headnotes have been written by scholars, with an eye to introducing students to the life and times of the author under discussion, paying attention to historical context as well, and making sure to prepare the way for the selection that follows. The footnotes provide useful glosses on words and phrases, keying the reader to certain historical moments or ideas, explaining oddities, offering extra material to make the texts more accessible.

Each of these themes is drawn from *The Wadsworth Anthology of American Literature,* which is scheduled for later publication. The first sequence of booklets, edited by Ralph Bauer at the University of Maryland, takes in the colonial period, which runs from the arrival of Columbus in the New World through 1820, a period of immense fluidity and dynamic cultural exchange. Bauer is a pioneering scholar who takes a hemispheric approach to the era, looking at the crush of cultures—Spanish, English, Dutch, German, French; each of these European powers sent colonial missions across the Atlantic Ocean, and the collision of these cultures with each other and with the Native American population (itself diverse and complicated) was combustive. Bauer isolates several themes, one of which is called "Between Cultures," and looks at the confrontation of European and Native American traditions. In "Spirituality, Church, and State in Colonial America," he examines the obsession with religious ideas, some of which led to the crisis in Salem, where the infamous witch trials occurred. In "Empire,

Science, and the Economy in the Americas," the focus shifts to the material basis for culture, and how it affected some outlying regions, such as Barbados, Peru, Mexico, and Alaska—thus blasting apart the rigid ways that scholars have more traditionally thought about North America in isolation. In "Contested Nations in the Early Americas," Bauer centers on revolutionary fervor in places like Haiti, Cuba, and Jamaica, where various groups fought for control of both territory and cultural influence.

In the second sequence of booklets, Shirley Samuels (who is Professor of English and American Studies at Cornell and has established herself as a major voice in the field of nineteenth-century American literature) looks at the early days of the American republic, a period stretching from 1800 to 1865, taking us through the Civil War. This was, of course, a period of huge expansion as well as consolidation. Manifest Destiny was a catchword, as the original thirteen colonies expanded in what Robert Frost referred to as "a nation gradually realizing westward." The question of identity arose on different fronts, and we see the beginnings of the women's movement here. In her first theme, Samuels looks at "The Woman Question," offering a selection of texts by men and women thinking about the place of a woman in society and in the home. Some of this writing is quite provocative, and much of it is rarely studied in college classrooms.

The racial questions came into focus during this era, too, and the groundwork for the Civil War was unhappily laid. In "Confronting Race," Samuels offers a searing medley of texts from Black Hawk through Frances E. W. Harper. These works hurl this topic into stark relief against a cultural landscape in perpetual ferment. This booklet includes selections from the speeches of Sojourner Truth, the pseudonym of an astonishing black woman, a former slave who became a leading abolitionist and advocate for women's rights.

In "Manifest Destiny and the Quest for the West," Samuels offers a mix of classic and lesser known texts on the theme of westward expansion, beginning with the remarkable *Journals of Lewis and Clark*, a key document in the literature of westward expansion and a vivid example of the literature of exploration. She ends with "Views of War," presenting a range of inspiring and heart-rending texts from a time of bloodshed, hatred, and immense idealism. The Union was very nearly broken, and one gets a full sense of the dynamics of this troubled era by comparing these texts by an unusual range of authors from Oliver Wendell Holmes and Julia Ward Howe through Sidney Lanier, one of the finest (if lesser known) poets of the era.

In the third sequence of booklets, Alfred Bendixen, who teaches at Texas A&M University, offers a selection from the period just after the Civil War through the beginnings of the modern period. Bendixen, who presides over the American Literature Association, has proven himself a scholar of unusual talents, and he brings his deep knowledge of the period into play here. In "Imagining Gender," he takes up where Samuels left off, looking at a compelling range of texts by men and women who consider the evolving issue of gender in fascinating ways. One sees the coalescing of the women's movement in some of this work, and also the resistance that inevitably arose, as women tried to assert themselves and to find their voice.

In "Questions of Social and Economic Justice," Bendixen puts forward texts by a range of key figures, including George Washington Cable, Hamlin Garland, Mary Wilkins Freeman, and Jack London. Each of these gifted writers meditates on the struggle of a young nation to define itself, to locate its economic pulse, to balance the need for economic expansion and development with the requirements and demands of social justice. Many of these themes carry forward into the twentieth century, and it is worth looking closely at the origins of these themes in an era of compulsive growth. Needless to say, this was also a period when millions of immigrants arrived from Southern and Eastern Europe, radically changing the complexion of the nation. Bendixen offers a unique blend of texts on the conflicts and questions that naturally followed the so-called Great Migration in "Immigration, Ethnicity, and Race." This section includes excerpts from Jane Addams's remarkable memoir of her time at Hull-House, a mansion in Chicago where she and her coworkers offered a range of social assistance and cultural programs to working class immigrants.

The most unusual theme in this sequence of booklets by Bendixen is "Crime, Mystery, and Detection." Here the student will find an array of gripping stories by some of the original authors in a field that forms the basis for contemporary popular fiction around the world. American readers in this period loved detective stories, and readers still do. The mix is quite unusual, and it remains fascinating to see how the genre found its legs and began to run, through a time when readers wished to apply all the tools of intelligence to their world, discovering its ways and meaning, trying to figure out "who done it" in so many ways.

Martha J. Cutter—a scholar of considerable range and achievement who now teaches at the University of Connecticut—edits the sequence of booklets dealing with the modern era, 1910–1945, a period of huge importance in American history and culture. The American empire came into its own in this era, recognized its muscles, and began to flex them—in ways productive and (at times) destructive. Cutter begins by looking at the women's movement, and how men reacted to certain inevitable pressures. In "The Making of the New Woman and the New Man," she charts the struggle between the sexes in a compelling range of texts, including works by Sui Sin Far, Edwin Arlington Robinson, James Weldon Johnson, Willa Cather, and John Steinbeck, among others. Of course, the subject of class had a massive impact on how people viewed themselves, and in "Modernism and the Literary Left," she presents a selection of works that deal with issues of class, money, and power. At the center of this sequence lies "May Day," one of F. Scott Fitzgerald's most luminous and provocative stories.

The New Negro Renaissance occurred during this period, a revival and consolidation of writing in a variety of genres by African Americans. Here Cutter offers a brilliant selection of key texts from this movement, including work by Langston Hughes and Zora Neale Hurston in "Racism and Activism." This booklet extends well beyond the Harlem Renaissance itself to work by Richard Wright, a major voice in African American literature.

As it must, the theme of war occupies a central place in one thematic booklet. In the first half of the twentieth century, world wars destroyed the lives of millions. Never had the world seen killing like this, or inhumanity and cruelty on a scale that beggars the imagination. The violence of these conflicts, and the cultural implications of such destruction, necessarily held the attention of major writers. And so, in "Poetry and Fiction of War and Social Conflict," we find a range of compelling work by such writers as Ezra Pound, H.D. (Hilda Doolittle), T. S. Eliot, and Edna St. Vincent Millay.

Henry Hart is a contemporary poet, biographer, and critic with a broad range of work to his credit (he holds a chair in literature at William and Mary College). His themes are drawn from the postwar era, and he puts before readers a seductive range of work by poets, fiction writers, and essayists. Many of the themes from earlier volumes continue here. For instance, Hart begins with "Race and Ethnicity in the Melting Pot," offering students a chance to think hard about the matter of ethnicity and race in contemporary America. With texts by James Baldwin and Malcolm X through Amy Tan and Ana Menéndez, he presents viewpoints that will prove challenging and provocative—perfect vehicles for classroom discussion.

In "Class Conflicts and the American Dream," Hart explores unstable, challenging terrain in a sequence of texts by major postwar authors from Martin Luther King, Jr. through Flannery O'Connor. Some of these works are extremely well known, such as John Updike's story, "A & P." Others, such as James Merrill's "The Broken Home" may be less familiar. This booklet, as a whole, provides a rich field of texts, and will stimulate discussion on many levels about the role of class in American society.

Similarly, Hart puts forward texts that deal with gender and sexuality in "Exploring Gender and Sexual Norms." From Sylvia Plath's wildly destructive poem about her father, "Daddy," through the anguished meditations in poetry of Adrienne Rich, Anne Sexton, Allen Ginsberg, and Frank O'Hara (among others), the complexities of sexuality and relationships emerge. In Gore Vidal's witty and ferocious look at homosexuality and anti-Semitism in "Pink Triangle and Yellow Star," students have an opportunity to think hard about things that are rarely put forward in frank terms. Further meditations on masculinity and as well as gay and lesbian sexualities occur in work by Pat Califia, Robert Bly, and Mark Doty. The section called "Witnessing War" offers some remarkable poems and stories by such writers as Robert Lowell, James Dickey, and Tim O'Brien—each of them writing from a powerful personal experience. In a medley of texts on "Religion and Spirituality," Hart explores connections to the sacred, drawing on work by such writers as Flannery O'Connor, Charles Wright, and Annie Dillard. As in earlier booklets, these thematic arrangements by Hart will challenge, entertain, and instruct.

In sum, we believe these booklets will stimulate conversations in class that should be productive as well as memorable, for teacher and student alike. The texts have been chosen because of their inherent interest and readability, and—in a sense—for the multiple ways in which they "talk" to each other. Culture is, of course, nothing more than good conversation, its elevation to a level of discourse. We, the editors of these thematic booklets, believe that the attractive arrangements of compelling texts will make a lasting impression, and will help to answer the question posed at the outset: What is America?

ACKNOWLEDGMENTS

We would like to thank the following readers and scholars who helped us shape this series: Brian Adler, Valdosta State University; John Alberti, Northern Kentucky University; Lee Alexander, College of William and Mary; Althea Allard, Community College of Rhode Island; Jonathan Barron, University of Southern Mississippi; Laura Behling, Gustavus Adolphus College; Peter Bellis, University of Alabama at Birmingham; Alan Belsches, Troy University Dothan Campus; Renee Bergland, Simmons College; Roy Bird, University of Alaska Fairbanks; Michael Borgstrom, San Diego State University; Patricia Bostian, Central Peidmont Community College; Jessica Bozek, Boston University; Lenore Brady, Arizona State University; Maria Brandt, Monroe Community College; Martin Buinicki, Valparaiso University; Stuart Burrows, Brown University; Shawrence Campbell, Stetson University; Steven Canaday, Anne Arundel Community College; Carole Chapman, Ivy Tech Community College of Indiana; Cheng Lok Chua, California State University; Philip Clark, McLean High School; Matt Cohen, Duke University; Patrick Collins, Austin Community College; Paul Cook, Arizona State University; Dean Cooledge, University of Maryland Eastern Shore; Howard Cox, Angelina College; Laura Cruse, Northwest Iowa Community College; Ed Dauterich, Kent State University; Janet Dean, Bryant University; Rebecca Devers, University of Connecticut; Joseph Dewey, University of Pittsburgh–Johnstown; Christopher Diller, Berry College; Elizabeth Donely, Clark College; Stacey Donohue, Central Oregon Community College; Douglas Dowland, The University of Iowa; Jacqueline Doyle, California State University, East Bay; Robert Dunne, Central Connecticut State University; Jim Egan, Brown University; Marcus Embry, University of Northern Colorado; Nikolai Endres, Western Kentucky University; Terry Engebretsen, Idaho State University; Jean Filetti, Christopher Newport University; Gabrielle Foreman, Occidental College; Luisa Forrest, El Centro College; Elizabeth Freeman, University of California Davis; Stephanie Freuler, Valencia Community College; Andrea Frisch, University of Maryland; Joseph Fruscione, Georgetown University; Lisa Giles, University of Southern Maine; Charles Gongre, Lamar State College–Port Arthur;

Gary Grieve-Carlson, Lebanon Valley College; Judy Harris, Tomball College; Brian Henry, University of Richmond; Allan Hikida, Seattle Central Community College; Lynn Houston, California State University, Chico; Coleman Hutchison, University of Texas–Austin; Andrew Jewell, University of Nebraska–Lincoln; Marion Kane, Lake-Sumter Community College; Laura Knight, Mercer County Community College; Delia Konzett, University of New Hampshire; Jon Little, Alverno College; Chris Lukasik, Purdue University; Martha B. Macdonald, York Technical College; Angie Macri, Pulaski Technical College; John Marsh, University of Illinois at Urbana Champaign; Christopher T. McDermot, University of Alabama; Jim McWilliams, Dickinson State University; Joe Mills, North Carolina School of the Arts; Bryan Moore, Arkansas State University; James Nagel, University of Georgia; Wade Newhouse, Peace College; Keith Newlin, University of North Carolina Wilmington; Andrew Newman, Stony Brook University; Brian Norman, Idaho State University; Scott Orme, Spokane Community College; Chris Phillips, Lafayette College; Jessica Rabin, Anne Arundel Community College; Audrey Raden, Hunter College; Catherine Rainwater, St. Edward's University; Rick Randolph, Kaua; Joan Reeves, Northeast Alabama Community College; Paul Reich, Rollins College; Yelizaveta Renfro, University of Nebraska–Lincoln; Roman Santillan, College of Staten Island; Marc Schuster, Montgomery County Community College; Carol Singley, Rutgers–Camden; Brenda Siragusa, Corinthian Colleges Inc.; John Staunton, University of North Caroline–Charlotte; Ryan Stryffeler, Ivy Tech Community College of Indiana; Robert Sturr, Kent State University, Stark Campus; James Tanner, University of North Texas; Alisa Thomas, Toccoa Falls College; Nathan Tipton, The University of Memphis; Gary Totten, North Dakota State University; Tony Trigilio, Columbia College, Chicago; Pat Tyrer, West Texas A&M University; Becky Villarreal, Austin Community College; Edward Walkiewicz, Oklahoma State University; Jay Watson, University of Mississippi; Karen Weekes, Penn State Abington; Bruce Weiner, St. Lawrence University; Cindy Weinstein, California Institute of Technology; Stephanie Wells, Orange Coast College; Robert West, Mississippi State University; Diane Whitley Bogard, Austin Community College–Eastview Campus; Edlie Wong, Rutgers; and Beth Younger, Drake University.

In addition, we would like to thank the indefatigable staff at Cengage Learning/Wadsworth for their tireless efforts to make these booklets and the upcoming anthology a reality: Michael Rosenberg, Publisher; Michell Phifer, Senior Development Editor, Lianne Ames, Senior Content Project Manager, Megan Garvey, Assistant Editor; Rebekah Matthews, Editorial Assistant, Emily Ryan, Associate Development Project Manager, Mandee Eckersley, Managing Marketing Manager, Stacey Purviance, Marketing Communications Manager, and Cate Barr, Art Director. We would also like to thank Kathy Smith, Project Manager, for her patience and attention to detail.

—Jay Parini, Middlebury College

Race and Ethnicity in the Melting Pot

Knowing the Other

Reflecting on the state of African Americans at the end of the twentieth century in *Race Matters*, the African American author Cornel West offered a bleak prognosis. "We have created rootless, dangling people with little link to the supportive networks—family, friends, school—that sustain some sense of purpose in life," he said. "We have witnessed the collapse of the spiritual communities that in the past helped Americans face despair, disease, and death and that transmit through the generations dignity and decency, excellence and elegance." Postmodern culture, with its "gangster mentalities and self-destructive wantonness," according to West, was partly to blame for the collapse. So was "a political atmosphere in which images, not ideas, dominate, where politicians spend more time raising money than debating issues." To cure the ills of racial and ethnic communities, West, like Martin Luther King, Jr., proposed a return to the fundamental principles of freedom and equality outlined in the Declaration of Independence. He also called for "a visionary leadership that can motivate 'the better angels of our nature.'" To go forward, West declared, America had to go back to its roots.

Writers with social consciences remind us that political change is local: it begins in the home; in personal relationships; in schools, churches, and communities. It begins with the sort of stirring, down-to-earth, and ultimately life-changing communication Gwendolyn Brooks offers in her poem "To the Young Who Want To Die." Brooks addresses the self-destructive impulses in unspecified young people, but she could be talking to and about her African American community. She appeals to "the better angels" of that community—its principles of life and creativity—as she tries to convince her audience to renounce suicide and destruction. She doesn't ignore the forces that afflict her community with pain and death. Rather, she affirms the opposite, spring-like forces that can bring new life to the waste land.

Political writers remind us that change depends on a keen knowledge of others, which in turn depends on open-mindedness and compassion. James Baldwin, Malcolm X, Gwendolyn Brooks, Rita Dove, Sherman Alexie, Amy Tan, Richard Rodriguez, and Ana Menéndez exercise the sort of sympathetic imagination needed to cure racial and ethnic problems even while pointing to the imagination's limits. They celebrate expression—musical, literary, political—as liberating and consoling, but they show how language in its broadest sense can misrepresent, isolate, and demean.

Menéndez's story about Cuban and Dominican exiles in Miami, Florida, involves epistemological questions as well. How can the tour guides and tourists who gawk at the exiles playing dominoes in the park really know them and their pasts? According to the main character Máximo, the guides' speeches and the tourists' photographs reduce the exiles to quaint stereotypes. Máximo's jokes both reveal and conceal the real suffering he experienced in Cuba. His last command regarding the tourists—"Tell them, no pictures"—is his declaration of independence from those who repeatedly misrepresent him. He demands to represent himself as he sees fit, and refuses to be turned into another sentimental image by Americans who know little or nothing about his difficult ethnic past.

Sonny in Baldwin's story feels similar resentments and makes similar demands. Rather than express his suffering in jokes, he finds his outlet for self-expression in music—in the blues. His brother, a schoolteacher, struggles to understand Sonny's work as a jazz musician. He wants to probe "the life that Sonny lived inside," but must get over his conventional attitudes to do so. "Sonny's Blues" is essentially a story about the art of listening. Sonny learns how to listen to the demonic "roar rising from the void" inside himself and triumphs by "imposing order on it as it hits the air." Sonny's brother's triumph comes when he finally listens to Sonny's music with insight and compassion. The epiphany is liberating and healing; it unites the once divided brothers. Sonny's brother concludes: "Freedom lurked around us and I understood, at last, that he could help us to be free if we would listen, that he would never be free until we did." Unlike Máximo and the tourists, the two brothers ultimately communicate with and understand each other.

Declarations of Independence

Post-World War II writers offer various declarations of independence and interpretations of freedom in their works. In "The Ballot or the Bullet," Malcolm X declares his independence from the U.S. and pledges his allegiance to Black Nationalism. He says he doesn't consider himself an American because he realizes that the foundational principles of America—"that all men are created equal, that they are endowed by their Creator with certain unalienable Rights"—do not apply to him. He welcomes allies in the effort to make black communities self-reliant, but his disillusionment with American democracy is palpable throughout his address. His disillusionment with King's nonviolent manner of protesting racial injustice is also palpable. Sometimes, the only way to rectify violent oppression, he argues, is with violence.

Although Rita Dove's "Wingfoot Lake," which takes place on Independence Day near the beginning of the Civil Rights Movement, acknowledges the ongoing presence of inequality and segregation in America, it also looks forward to an end to the sort of longstanding injustices that Malcolm X describes. Although Dove's grandmother, Beulah, feels threatened by the rapidly changing times, Beulah's offspring are caught up in the heady possibilities of racial progress. They don't view King's march on Washington, D.C. as an ominous sign of an impending race war, but rather as a sign of a better future for African Americans.

Conflicts and reunions figure into Sherman Alexie's story about a Native American father who hears, and then becomes obsessed with, Jimi Hendrix's version of "The Star-Spangled Banner" at the Woodstock rock concert in 1969. By playing variations on the national anthem, which recalls violent American struggles for freedom in the past ("the rockets' red glare, the bombs bursting in air"), Hendrix declares independence from the bloodshed and failed promises that have littered American history. Hendrix's rendition of the anthem becomes a powerful elixir for the Indian because it sums up the vacillations between violence and peace in his life, community, and country. Battles for independence are all he has really known. His son, Victor, who narrates the story, expresses the sadness that results from his father's turbulent attempts to be free.

Broken ethnic families and communities haunt the writings of Tan and Rodriguez as well. In Tan's story, Chinese families make painful sacrifices to leave a country they associate with bondage (China) for a country they associate with freedom and opportunity (the United States). The characters, who do their best to blend into the melting pot and achieve the American dream, wonder if their arduous pursuits of freedom and happiness are worth it. "All those sacrifices to bring so much unhappiness to America!" one character exclaims. In America, a Chinese mother is disappointed that her daughter never visits her; another frets that her son, who was initially left behind in Formosa, does little more than smoke, play video games, and eat. Divided from their homes in China, Tan's families continue to suffer. They learn "how something can still hurt you after it's gone," how independence in an alien culture comes at a painful price.

Rodriguez gives a more auspicious account of the ethnic alien's plunge into the American melting pot, but he, too, recognizes the price. Speaking Spanish as a child with his Mexican family convinced him that his home was a sanctuary. When his parents spoke faltering English, he felt their "protection and power" diminish. As he grew up, however, "having to learn the language of public society"—English—allowed him opportunities he never would have had as a mere Spanish speaker. He learned to respect "the value and necessity of assimilation." The real boons of freedom come when he declares independence from the smaller community of his family to join the larger community of America. The price he pays—the loss of family harmony, the growing silence of his parents—is worth it, he concludes.

Unlike some of the characters in the stories and poems of his contemporaries, Rodriguez enjoys a happy end to his quest for the American dream. He manages to reconcile the desires for independence and unity by sacrificing private nostalgia for his Hispanic roots and accepting a public role in American society. Rather than dwell on the continuing hardships of racial and ethnic injustice, he points to the achievable benefits of assimilation. In short, he maintains his faith in the American dream. He still believes that liberty and justice are possible for all.

James Baldwin 1924–1987

A prolific and versatile African American writer, James Baldwin created a rich body of work, including novels, essays, short stories, poems, a children's book, and a movie script. Many of his books were bestsellers in the United States and Europe. He was known as an ardent critic of American racism.

Baldwin was born in Harlem to an unmarried mother, Emma Berdis Jones, who married David Baldwin when her son was three. He grew up in poverty with eight siblings. Baldwin had a tense relationship with his stepfather, a storefront preacher who had an Old Testament vision of an angry God. Baldwin's later work would show the stamp of these early teachings, exhibiting a blend of the African American rhythms he heard in spirituals and gospel songs. In high school, Baldwin became involved with the school newspaper and literary club. He left Harlem after high school, worked for a time in New Jersey, then moved to Greenwich Village in New York, where the writer Richard Wright helped him to receive a Eugene F. Saxton Memorial Trust Award to work on his first novel, the semi-autobiographical *Go Tell It on the Mountain* (1953), which explores the relationship between a young boy and his preacher father.

In 1948, Baldwin moved to Paris, one year after Wright made the same journey. Baldwin returned to the United States in 1957 to take part in the Civil Rights struggle, but he later went back to Paris and spent most of his last years there. Baldwin's honors include a Guggenheim Fellowship, a Ford Foundation Grant-in-Aid, and a National Institute of Arts and Letters Fellowship. He taught at the University of Massachusetts at Amherst and Hampshire College. Baldwin died in St. Paul de Vence, France, in 1987.

The short story "Sonny's Blues" was first published in 1957 in the *Partisan Review*. The narrator of the story is a husband and father struggling with his own life and with his responsibility to his younger musician brother, Sonny. In the climax of the story, the narrator has a revelation in which he sees that Sonny, as a black musician, is struggling for freedom. The exploration of the relationship between two brothers is a theme that occurs elsewhere in Baldwin's fiction, including the novels *Tell Me How Long the Train's Been Gone* (1968) and *Just Above My Head* (1979).

As a gay writer, Baldwin explored homosexuality in several of his novels, including *Giovanni's Room* (1956) and *Another Country* (1962). His novel *If Beale Street Could Talk* (1974) focuses on heterosexual love and a young black couple's struggle to stay together and become a family. Baldwin was also an acclaimed essay writer. His essay collections include *Notes of a Native Son* (1955), *Nobody Knows My Name* (1961), *The Fire Next Time* (1963), *The Devil Finds Work* (1976), *The Evidence of Things Not Seen* (1985), and *The Price of the Ticket: Collected Nonfiction, 1948–1985* (1985).

Further Reading Fern Marja Eckman, *The Furious Passage of James Baldwin* (1966); Trudier Harris, *Black Women in the Fiction of James Baldwin* (1985); Horace A. Porter, *Stealing the Fire: The Art and Protest of James Baldwin* (1989); James Campbell, *Talking at the Gates: A Life of James Baldwin* (1991).

—*Yelizaveta P. Renfro, University of Nebraska*

Sonny's Blues

I read about it in the paper, in the subway, on my way to work. I read it, and I couldn't believe it, and I read it again. Then perhaps I just stared at it, at the newsprint spelling out his name, spelling out the story. I stared at it in the swinging lights of the subway car, and in the faces and bodies of the people, and in my own face, trapped in the darkness which roared outside.

It was not to be believed and I kept telling myself that, as I walked from the subway station to the high school. And at the same time I couldn't doubt it. I was scared, scared for Sonny. He became real to me again. A great block of ice got settled in my belly and kept melting there slowly all day long, while I taught my classes algebra. It was a special kind of ice. It kept melting, sending trickles of ice water all up and down my veins, but it never got less. Sometimes it hardened and seemed to expand until I felt my guts were going to come spilling out or that I was going to choke or scream. This would always be at a moment when I was remembering some specific thing Sonny had once said or done.

When he was about as old as the boys in my classes his face had been bright and open, there was a lot of copper in it; and he'd had wonderfully direct brown eyes, and great gentleness and privacy. I wondered what he looked like now. He had been picked up, the evening before, in a raid on an apartment downtown, for peddling and using heroin.

I couldn't believe it: but what I mean by that is that I couldn't find any room for it anywhere inside me. I had kept it outside me for a long time. I hadn't wanted to know. I had had suspicions, but I didn't name them, I kept putting them away. I told myself that Sonny was wild, but he wasn't crazy. And he'd always been a good boy, he hadn't ever turned hard or evil or disrespectful, the way kids can, so quick, so quick, especially in Harlem. I didn't want to believe that I'd ever see my brother going down, coming to nothing, all that light in his face gone out, in the condition I'd already seen so many others. Yet it had happened and here I was, talking about algebra to a lot of boys who might, every one of them for all I knew, be popping off needles every time they went to the head. Maybe it did more for them than algebra could.

I was sure that the first time Sonny had ever had horse, he couldn't have been much older than these boys were now. These boys, now, were living as we'd been living then, they were growing up with a rush and their heads bumped abruptly against the low ceiling of their actual possibilities. They were filled with rage. All they really knew were two darknesses, the darkness of their lives, which was now closing in on them, and the darkness of the movies, which had blinded them to that other darkness, and in which they now, vindictively, dreamed, at once more together than they were at any other time, and more alone.

When the last bell rang, the last class ended, I let out my breath. It seemed I'd been holding it for all that time. My clothes were wet—I may have looked as though I'd been sitting in a steam bath, all dressed up, all afternoon. I sat alone in the classroom a long time. I listened to the boys outside, downstairs, shouting and cursing and laughing. Their laughter struck me for perhaps the first time. It was not the joyous laughter which—God knows why—one associates with children. It was mocking and insular, its intent to denigrate. It was disenchanted, and in this, also, lay the authority of their curses. Perhaps I was listening to them because I was thinking about my brother and in them I heard my brother. And myself.

One boy was whistling a tune, at once very complicated and very simple, it seemed to be pouring out of him as though he were a bird, and it sounded very cool and moving through all that harsh, bright air, only just holding its own through all those other sounds.

I stood up and walked over to the window and looked down into the courtyard. It was the beginning of the spring and the sap was rising in the boys. A teacher passed through them every now and again, quickly, as though he or she couldn't wait to get out of that courtyard, to get those boys out of their sight and off their minds. I started collecting my stuff. I thought I'd better get home and talk to Isabel.

The courtyard was almost deserted by the time I got downstairs. I saw this boy standing in the shadow of a doorway, looking just like Sonny. I almost called his name. Then I saw that it wasn't Sonny, but somebody we used to know, a boy from around our block. He'd been Sonny's friend. He'd never been mine, having been too young for me, and, anyway, I'd never liked him. And now, even though he was a grown-up man, he still hung around that block, still spent hours on the street corners, was always high and raggy. I used to run into him from time to time and he'd often work around to asking me for a quarter or fifty cents. He always had some real good excuse, too, and I always gave it to him, I don't know why.

But now, abruptly, I hated him. I couldn't stand the way he looked at me, partly like a dog, partly like a cunning child. I wanted to ask him what the hell he was doing in the school courtyard.

He sort of shuffled over to me, and he said, "I see you got the papers. So you already know about it."

"You mean about Sonny? Yes, I already know about it. How come they didn't get you?"

He grinned. It made him repulsive and it also brought to mind what he'd looked like as a kid. "I wasn't there. I stay away from them people."

"Good for you." I offered him a cigarette and I watched him through the smoke. "You come all the way down here just to tell me about Sonny?"

"That's right." He was sort of shaking his head and his eyes looked strange, as though they were about to cross. The bright sun deadened his damp dark brown skin and it made his eyes look yellow and showed up the dirt in his kinked hair. He smelled funky. I moved a little away from him and I said, "Well, thanks. But I already know about it and I got to get home."

"I'll walk you a little ways," he said. We started walking. There were a couple of kids still loitering in the courtyard and one of them said goodnight to me and looked strangely at the boy beside me.

"What're you going to do?" he asked me. "I mean, about Sonny?"

"Look. I haven't seen Sonny for over a year, I'm not sure I'm going to do anything. Anyway, what the hell *can* I do?"

"That's right," he said quickly, "ain't nothing you can do. Can't much help old Sonny no more, I guess."

It was what I was thinking and so it seemed to me he had no right to say it.

"I'm surprised at Sonny, though," he went on—he had a funny way of talking, he looked straight ahead as though he were talking to himself—"I thought Sonny was a smart boy, I thought he was too smart to get hung."

"I guess he thought so too," I said sharply, "and that's how he got hung. And now about you? You're pretty goddamn smart, I bet."

Then he looked directly at me, just for a minute. "I ain't smart," he said. "If I was smart, I'd have reached for a pistol a long time ago."

"Look. Don't tell *me* your sad story, if it was up to me, I'd give you one." Then I felt guilty—guilty, probably, for never having supposed that the poor bastard *had* a story of his own, much less a sad one, and I asked, quickly, "What's going to happen to him now?"

He didn't answer this. He was off by himself some place. "Funny thing," he said, and from his tone we might have been discussing the quickest way to get to Brooklyn, "when I saw the papers this morning, the first thing I asked myself was if I had anything to do with it. I felt sort of responsible."

I began to listen more carefully. The subway station was on the corner, just before us, and I stopped. He stopped, too. We were in front of a bar and he ducked slightly, peering in, but whoever he was looking for didn't seem to be there. The juke box was blasting away with something black and bouncy and I half watched the barmaid as she danced her way from the juke box to her place behind the bar. And I watched her face as she laughingly responded to something someone said to her, still keeping time to the music. When she smiled one saw the little girl, one sensed the doomed, still-struggling woman beneath the battered face of the semi-whore.

"I never *give* Sonny nothing," the boy said finally, "but a long time ago I come to school high and Sonny asked me how it felt." He paused, I couldn't bear to watch him, I watched the barmaid, and I listened to the music which seemed to be causing the pavement to shake. "I told him it felt great." The music stopped, the barmaid paused and watched the juke box until the music began again. "It did."

All this was carrying me some place I didn't want to go. I certainly didn't want to know how it felt. It filled everything, the people, the houses, the music, the dark, quicksilver barmaid, with menace; and this menace was their reality.

"What's going to happen to him now?" I asked again.

"They'll send him away some place and they'll try to cure him." He shook his head. "Maybe he'll even think he's kicked the habit. Then they'll let him loose"—he gestured, throwing his cigarette into the gutter. "That's all."

"What do you mean, that's *all*?"

But I knew what he meant.

"I *mean*, that's *all*." He turned his head and looked at me, pulling down the corners of his mouth. "Don't you know what I mean?" he asked, softly.

"How the hell *would* I know what you mean?" I almost whispered it, I don't know why.

"That's right," he said to the air, "how would *he* know what I mean?" He turned toward me again, patient and calm, and yet I somehow felt him shaking, shaking as though he were going to fall apart. I felt that ice in my guts again, the dread I'd felt all afternoon; and again I watched the barmaid, moving about the bar, washing glasses, and singing. "Listen. They'll let him out and then it'll just start all over again. That's what I mean."

"You mean—they'll let him out. And then he'll just start working his way back in again. You mean he'll never kick the habit. Is that what you mean?"

"That's right," he said, cheerfully. "*You* see what I mean."

"Tell me," I said at last, "why does he want to die? He must want to die, he's killing himself, why does he want to die?"

He looked at me in surprise. He licked his lips. "He don't want to die. He wants to live. Don't nobody want to die, ever."

Then I wanted to ask him—too many things. He could not have answered, or if he had, I could not have borne the answers. I started walking. "Well, I guess it's none of my business."

"It's going to be rough on old Sonny," he said. We reached the subway station. "This is your station?" he asked. I nodded. I took one step down. "Damn!" he said, suddenly. I looked up at him. He grinned again. "Damn it if I didn't leave all my money home. You ain't got a dollar on you, have you? Just for a couple of days, is all."

All at once something inside gave and threatened to come pouring out of me. I didn't hate him any more. I felt that in another moment I'd start crying like a child.

"Sure," I said. "Don't sweat." I looked in my wallet and didn't have a dollar, I only had a five. "Here," I said. "That hold you?"

He didn't look at it—he didn't want to look at it. A terrible closed look came over his face, as though he were keeping the number on the bill a secret from him and me. "Thanks," he said, and now he was dying to see me go. "Don't worry about Sonny. Maybe I'll write him or something."

"Sure," I said. "You do that. So long."

"Be seeing you," he said. I went on down the steps.

And I didn't write Sonny or send him anything for a long time. When I finally did, it was just after my little girl died, he wrote me back a letter which made me feel like a bastard.

Here's what he said:

Dear brother,

You don't know how much I needed to hear from you. I wanted to write you many a time but I dug how much I must have hurt you and so I didn't write. But now I feel like a man who's been trying to climb up out of some deep, real deep and funky hole and just saw the sun up there, outside. I got to get outside.

I can't tell you much about how I got here. I mean I don't know how to tell you. I guess I was afraid of something or I was trying to escape from something and you know I have never been very strong in the head (smile). I'm glad Mama and Daddy are dead and can't see what's happened to their son and I swear if I'd known what I was doing I would never have hurt you so, you and a lot of other fine people who were nice to me and who believed in me.

I don't want you to think it had anything to do with me being a musician. It's more than that. Or maybe less than that. I can't get anything straight in my head down here and I try not to think about what's going to happen to me when I get outside again. Sometime I think I'm going to flip and *never* get outside and sometime I think I'll come straight back. I tell you one thing, though, I'd rather blow my brains out than go through this again. But that's what they all say, so they tell me. If I tell you when I'm coming to New York and if you could meet me, I sure would appreciate it. Give my love to Isabel and the kids and I was sure sorry to hear about little Gracie. I wish I could be like Mama and say the Lord's will be done, but I don't know it seems to me that trouble is the one thing that never does get stopped and I don't know what good it does to blame it on the Lord. But maybe it does some good if you believe it.

Your brother,
Sonny

Then I kept in constant touch with him and I sent him whatever I could and I went to meet him when he came back to New York. When I saw him many things I thought I had forgotten came flooding back to me. This was because I had begun, finally, to wonder about Sonny, about the life that Sonny lived inside. This life, whatever it was, had made him older and thinner and it had deepened the distant stillness in which he had always moved. He looked very unlike my baby brother. Yet, when he smiled, when we shook hands, the baby brother I'd never known looked out from the depths of his private life, like an animal waiting to be coaxed into the light.

"How you been keeping?" he asked me.

"All right. And you?"

"Just fine." He was smiling all over his face. "It's good to see you again."

"It's good to see you."

The seven years difference in our ages lay between us like a chasm: I wondered if these years would ever operate between us as a bridge. I was remembering, and it made it hard to catch my breath, that I had been there when he was born; and I had heard the first words he had ever spoken. When he started to walk, he walked from our mother straight to me. I caught him just before he fell when he took the first steps he ever took in this world.

"How's Isabel?"

"Just fine. She's dying to see you."

"And the boys?"

"They're fine, too. They're anxious to see their uncle."

"Oh, come on. You know they don't remember me."

"Are you kidding? Of course they remember you."

He grinned again. We got into a taxi. We had a lot to say to each other, far too much to know how to begin.

As the taxi began to move, I asked, "You still want to go to India?"

He laughed. "You still remember that. Hell, no. This place is Indian enough for me."

"It used to belong to them," I said.

And he laughed again. "They damn sure knew what they were doing when they got rid of it."

Years ago, when he was around fourteen, he'd been all hipped on the idea of going to India. He read books about people sitting on rocks, naked, in all kinds of weather, but mostly bad, naturally, and walking barefoot through hot coals and arriving at wisdom. I used to say that it sounded to me as though they were getting away from wisdom as fast as they could. I think he sort of looked down on me for that.

"Do you mind," he asked, "if we have the driver drive alongside the park? On the west side—I haven't seen the city in so long."

"Of course not," I said. I was afraid that I might sound as though I were humoring him, but I hoped he wouldn't take it that way.

So we drove along, between the green of the park and the stony, lifeless elegance of hotels and apartment buildings, toward the vivid, killing streets of our childhood. These streets hadn't changed, though housing projects jutted up out of them now like rocks in the middle of a boiling sea. Most of the houses in which we had grown up had vanished, as had the stores from which we had stolen, the basements in which we had first tried sex, the rooftops from which we had hurled tin cans and bricks. But houses exactly like the houses of our past yet dominated the landscape, boys exactly like the boys we once had been found themselves smothering in these houses, came down into the streets for light and air and found themselves encircled by disaster. Some escaped the trap, most didn't. Those who got out always left something of themselves behind, as some animals amputate a leg and leave it in the trap. It might be said, perhaps, that I had escaped, after all, I was a school teacher; or that Sonny had, he hadn't lived in Harlem for years. Yet, as the cab moved uptown through streets which seemed, with a rush, to darken with dark people, and as I covertly studied Sonny's face, it came to me that what we both were seeking through our separate cab windows was that part of ourselves which had been left behind. It's always at the hour of trouble and confrontation that the missing member aches.

We hit 110th Street and started rolling up Lenox Avenue. And I'd known this avenue all my life, but it seemed to me again, as it had seemed on the day I'd first heard about Sonny's trouble, filled with a hidden menace which was its very breath of life.

"We almost there," said Sonny.

"Almost." We were both too nervous to say anything more.

We live in a housing project. It hasn't been up long. A few days after it was up it seemed uninhabitably new, now, of course, it's already rundown. It looks like a parody of the good, clean, faceless life—God knows the people who live in it do their best to make it a parody. The beat-looking grass lying around isn't enough to make their lives green, the hedges will never hold out the streets, and they know it. The big windows fool no one, they aren't big enough to make space out of no space. They don't bother with the windows, they watch the TV screen instead. The playground is most popular with the children who don't play at jacks, or skip rope, or roller skate, or swing, and they can be found in it after dark. We moved in partly because it's not too far from where I teach, and partly for the kids; but it's really just like the houses in which Sonny and I grew up. The same things happen, they'll have the same things to remember. The moment Sonny and I started into the house I had the feeling that I was simply bringing him back into the danger he had almost died trying to escape.

Sonny has never been talkative. So I don't know why I was sure he'd be dying to talk to me when supper was over the first night. Everything went fine, the oldest boy remembered him, and the youngest boy liked him, and Sonny had remembered to bring something for each of them; and Isabel, who is really much nicer than I am, more open and giving, had gone to a lot of trouble about dinner and was genuinely glad to see him. And she's always been able to tease Sonny in a way that I haven't. It was nice to see her face so vivid again and to hear her laugh and watch her make Sonny laugh. She wasn't, or, anyway, she didn't seem to be, at all uneasy or embarrassed. She chatted as though there were no subject which had to be avoided and she got Sonny past his first, faint stiffness. And thank God she was there, for I was filled with that icy dread again. Everything I did seemed awkward to me, and everything I said sounded freighted with hidden meaning. I was trying to remember everything I'd heard about dope addiction and I couldn't help watching Sonny for signs. I wasn't doing it out of malice. I was trying to find out something about my brother. I was dying to hear him tell me he was safe.

"Safe!" my father grunted, whenever Mama suggested trying to move to a neighborhood which might be safer for children. "Safe, hell! Ain't no place safe for kids, nor nobody."

He always went on like this, but he wasn't, ever, really as bad as he sounded, not even on weekends, when he got drunk. As a matter of fact, he was always on the lookout for "something a little better," but he died before he found it. He died suddenly, during a drunken weekend in the middle of the war, when Sonny was fifteen. He and Sonny hadn't ever got on too well. And this was partly because Sonny was the apple of his father's eye. It was because he loved Sonny so much and was frightened for him, that he was always fighting with him. It doesn't do any good to fight with Sonny. Sonny just moves back, inside himself, where he can't be reached. But the principal reason that they never hit it off is that they were so much alike. Daddy was big and rough and loud-talking, just the opposite of Sonny, but they both had—that same privacy.

Mama tried to tell me something about this, just after Daddy died. I was home on leave from the army.

This was the last time I ever saw my mother alive. Just the same, this picture gets all mixed up in my mind with pictures I had of her when she was younger. The way I always see her is the way she used to be on a Sunday afternoon, say, when the old folks were talking after the big Sunday dinner. I always see her wearing pale blue. She'd be sitting on the sofa. And my father would be sitting in the easy chair, not far from her. And the living room would be full of church folks and relatives. There they sit, in chairs all around the living room, and the night is creeping up outside, but nobody knows it yet. You can see the darkness growing against the windowpanes and you hear the street noises every now and again, or maybe the jangling beat of a tambourine from one of the churches close by, but it's real quiet in the room. For a moment nobody's talking, but every face looks darkening, like the sky outside. And my mother rocks a little from the waist, and my father's eyes are closed. Everyone is looking at something a child can't see. For a minute they've forgotten the children. Maybe a kid is lying on the rug, half asleep. Maybe somebody's got a kid in his lap and is absentmindedly stroking the kid's head. Maybe there's a kid, quiet and big-eyed, curled up in a big chair in the corner. The silence, the darkness coming, and the darkness in the faces frightens the child obscurely. He hopes that the hand which strokes his forehead will never stop—will never die. He hopes that there will never come a time when the old folks won't be sitting around the living room, talking about where they've come from, and what they've seen, and what's happened to them and their kinfolk.

But something deep and watchful in the child knows that this is bound to end, is already ending. In a moment someone will get up and turn on the light. Then the old folks will remember the children and they won't talk any more that day. And when light fills the room, the child is filled with darkness. He knows that everytime this happens he's moved just a little closer to that darkness outside. The darkness outside is what the old folks have been talking about. It's what they've come from. It's what they endure. The child knows that they won't talk any more because if he knows too much about what's happened to *them*, he'll know too much too soon, about what's going to happen to *him*.

The last time I talked to my mother, I remember I was restless. I wanted to get out and see Isabel. We weren't married then and we had a lot to straighten out between us.

There Mama sat, in black, by the window. She was humming an old church song, *Lord, you brought me from a long ways off*. Sonny was out somewhere. Mama kept watching the streets.

"I don't know," she said, "if I'll ever see you again, after you go off from here. But I hope you'll remember the things I tried to teach you."

"Don't talk like that," I said, and smiled. "You'll be here a long time yet."

She smiled, too, but she said nothing. She was quiet for a long time. And I said, "Mama, don't you worry about nothing. I'll be writing all the time, and you be getting the checks…."

"I want to talk to you about your brother," she said, suddenly. "If anything happens to me he ain't going to have nobody to look out for him."

"Mama," I said, "ain't nothing going to happen to you or Sonny. Sonny's all right. He's a good boy and he's got good sense."

"It ain't a question of his being a good boy," Mama said, "nor of his having good sense. It ain't only the bad ones, nor yet the dumb ones that gets sucked under." She stopped, looking at me. "Your Daddy once had a brother," she said, and she smiled in a way that made me feel she was in pain. "You didn't never know that, did you?"

"No," I said, "I never knew that," and I watched her face.

"Oh, yes," she said, "your Daddy had a brother." She looked out of the window again. "I know you never saw your Daddy cry. But I did—many a time, through all these years."

I asked her, "What happened to his brother? How come nobody's ever talked about him?"

This was the first time I ever saw my mother look old.

"His brother got killed," she said, "when he was just a little younger than you are now. I knew him. He was a fine boy. He was maybe a little full of the devil, but he didn't mean nobody no harm."

Then she stopped and the room was silent, exactly as it had sometimes been on those Sunday afternoons. Mama kept looking out into the streets.

"He used to have a job in the mill," she said, "and, like all young folks, he just liked to perform on Saturday nights. Saturday nights, him and your father would drift around to different places, go to dances and things like that, or just sit around with people they knew, and your father's brother would sing, he had a fine voice, and play along with himself on his guitar. Well, this particular Saturday night, him and your father was coming home from some place, and they were both a little drunk and there was a moon that night, it was bright like day. Your father's brother was feeling kind of good, and he was whistling to himself, and he had his guitar slung over his shoulder. They was coming down a hill and beneath them was a road that turned off from the highway. Well, your father's brother, being always kind of frisky, decided to run down this hill, and he did, with that guitar banging and clanging behind him, and he ran across the road, and he was making water behind a tree. And your father was sort of amused at him and he was still coming down the hill, kind of slow. Then he heard a car motor and that same minute his brother stepped from behind the tree, into the road, in the moonlight. And he started to cross the road. And your father started to run down the hill, he says he don't know why. This car was full of white men. They was all drunk, and when they seen your father's brother they let out a great whoop and holler and they aimed the car straight at him. They was having fun, they just wanted to scare him, the way they do sometimes, you know. But they was drunk. And I guess the boy, being drunk, too, and scared, kind of lost his head. By the time he jumped it was too late. Your father says he heard his brother scream when the car rolled over him, and he heard the wood of that guitar when it give, and he heard them strings go flying, and he heard them white men shouting, and the car kept on a-going and it ain't stopped till this day. And, time your father got down the hill, his brother weren't nothing but blood and pulp."

Tears were gleaming on my mother's face. There wasn't anything I could say.

"He never mentioned it," she said, "because I never let him mention it before you children. Your Daddy was like a crazy man that night and for many a night thereafter. He says he never in his life seen anything as dark as that road after the lights of that car had gone away. Weren't nothing, weren't nobody on that road, just your Daddy and his brother and that busted guitar. Oh, yes. Your Daddy never did really get right again. Till the day he died he weren't sure but that every white man he saw was the man that killed his brother."

She stopped and took out her handkerchief and dried her eyes and looked at me.

"I ain't telling you all this," she said, "to make you scared or bitter or to make you hate nobody. I'm telling you this because you got a brother. And the world ain't changed."

I guess I didn't want to believe this. I guess she saw this in my face. She turned away from me, toward the window again, searching those streets.

"But I praise my Redeemer," she said at last, "that He called your Daddy home before me. I ain't saying it to throw no flowers at myself, but, I declare, it keeps me from feeling too cast down to know I helped your father get safely through this world. Your father always acted like he was the roughest, strongest man on earth. And everybody took him to be like that. But if he hadn't had *me* there—to see his tears!"

She was crying again. Still, I couldn't move. I said, "Lord, Lord, Mama, I didn't know it was like that."

"Oh, honey," she said, "there's a lot that you don't know. But you are going to find it out." She stood up from the window and came over to me. "You got to hold on to your brother," she said, "and don't let him fall, no matter what it looks like is happening to him and no matter how evil you gets with him. You going to be evil with him many a time. But don't you forget what I told you, you hear?"

"I won't forget," I said. "Don't you worry, I won't forget. I won't let nothing happen to Sonny."

My mother smiled as though she were amused at something she saw in my face. Then, "You may not be able to stop nothing from happening. But you got to let him know you's *there*."

Two days later I was married, and then I was gone. And I had a lot of things on my mind and I pretty well forgot my promise to Mama until I got shipped home on a special furlough for her funeral.

And, after the funeral, with just Sonny and me alone in the empty kitchen, I tried to find out something about him.

"What do you want to do?" I asked him.

"I'm going to be a musician," he said.

For he had graduated, in the time I had been away, from dancing to the juke box to finding out who was playing what, and what they were doing with it, and he had bought himself a set of drums.

"You mean, you want to be a drummer?" I somehow had the feeling that being a drummer might be all right for other people but not for my brother Sonny.

"I don't think," he said, looking at me very gravely, "that I'll ever be a good drummer. But I think I can play a piano."

I frowned. I'd never played the role of the older brother quite so seriously before, had scarcely ever, in fact, *asked* Sonny a damn thing. I sensed myself in the presence of something I didn't really know how to handle, didn't understand. So

I made my frown a little deeper as I asked: "What kind of musician do you want to be?"

He grinned. "How many kinds do you think there are?"

"Be *serious*," I said.

He laughed, throwing his head back, and then looked at me. "I *am* serious."

"Well, then, for Christ's sake, stop kidding around and answer a serious question. I mean, do you want to be a concert pianist, you want to play classical music and all that, or—or what?" Long before I finished he was laughing again. "For Christ's *sake*, Sonny!"

He sobered, but with difficulty. "I'm sorry. But you sound so—*scared*!" and he was off again.

"Well, you may think it's funny now, baby, but it's not going to be so funny when you have to make your living at it, let me tell you *that*." I was furious because I knew he was laughing at me and I didn't know why

"No," he said, very sober now, and afraid, perhaps, that he'd hurt me, "I don't want to be a classical pianist. That isn't what interests me. I mean"—he paused, looking hard at me, as though his eyes would help me to understand, and then gestured helplessly, as though perhaps his hand would help—"I mean, I'll have a lot of studying to do, and I'll have to study everything, but, I mean, I want to play *with*— jazz musicians." He stopped. "I want to play jazz," he said.

Well, the word had never before sounded as heavy, as real, as it sounded that afternoon in Sonny's mouth. I just looked at him and I was probably frowning a real frown by this time. I simply couldn't see why on earth he'd want to spend his time hanging around nightclubs, clowning around on bandstands, while people pushed each other around a dance floor. It seemed—beneath him, somehow. I had never thought about it before, had never been forced to, but I suppose I had always put jazz musicians in a class with what Daddy called "good-time people."

"Are you *serious*?"

"Hell, *yes*, I'm serious."

He looked more helpless than ever, and annoyed, and deeply hurt.

I suggested, helpfully: "You mean—like Louis Armstrong?"

His face closed as though I'd struck him. "No. I'm not talking about none of that old-time, down home crap."

"Well, look, Sonny, I'm sorry, don't get mad. I just don't altogether get it, that's all. Name somebody—you know, a jazz musician you admire."

"Bird."

"Who?"

"Bird! Charlie Parker! Don't they teach you nothing in the goddamn army?"

I lit a cigarette. I was surprised and then a little amused to discover that I was trembling. "I've been out of touch," I said. "You'll have to be patient with me. Now. Who's this Parker character?"

"He's just one of the greatest jazz musicians alive," said Sonny, sullenly, his hands in his pockets, his back to me. "Maybe *the* greatest," he added, bitterly, "that's probably why *you* never heard of him."

"All right," I said, "I'm ignorant. I'm sorry. I'll go out and buy all the cat's records right away, all right?"

"It don't," said Sonny, with dignity, "make any difference to me. I don't care what you listen to. Don't do me no favors."

I was beginning to realize that I'd never seen him so upset before. With another part of my mind I was thinking that this would probably turn out to be one of those things kids go through and that I shouldn't make it seem important by pushing it too hard. Still, I didn't think it would do any harm to ask: "Doesn't all this take a lot of time? Can you make a living at it?"

He turned back to me and half leaned, half sat, on the kitchen table. "Everything takes time," he said, "and—well, yes, sure, I can make a living at it. But what I don't seem to be able to make you understand is that it's the only thing I want to do."

"Well, Sonny," I said, gently, "you know people can't always do exactly what they *want* to do—"

"*No*, I don't know that," said Sonny, surprising me. "I think people *ought* to do what they want to do, what else are they alive for?"

"You getting to be a big boy," I said desperately, "it's time you started thinking about your future."

"I'm thinking about my future," said Sonny, grimly. "I think about it all the time."

I gave up. I decided, if he didn't change his mind, that we could always talk about it later. "In the meantime," I said, "you got to finish school." We had already decided that he'd have to move in with Isabel and her folks. I knew this wasn't the ideal arrangement because Isabel's folks are inclined to be dicty and they hadn't especially wanted Isabel to marry me. But I didn't know what else to do. "And we have to get you fixed up at Isabel's."

There was a long silence. He moved from the kitchen table to the window. "That's a terrible idea. You know it yourself."

"Do you have a *better* idea?"

He just walked up and down the kitchen for a minute. He was as tall as I was. He had started to shave. I suddenly had the feeling that I didn't know him at all.

He stopped at the kitchen table and picked up my cigarettes. Looking at me with a kind of mocking, amused defiance, he put one between his lips. "You mind?"

"You smoking already?"

He lit the cigarette and nodded, watching me through the smoke. "I just wanted to see if I'd have the courage to smoke in front of you." He grinned and blew a great cloud of smoke to the ceiling. "It was easy." He looked at my face. "Come on, now. I bet you was smoking at my age, tell the truth."

I didn't say anything but the truth was on my face, and he laughed. But now there was something very strained in his laugh. "Sure. And I bet that ain't all you was doing."

He was frightening me a little. "Cut the crap," I said. "We already decided that you was going to go and live at Isabel's. Now what's got into you all of a sudden?"

"*You* decided it," he pointed out. "*I* didn't decide nothing." He stopped in front of me, leaning against the stove, arms loosely folded. "Look, brother. I don't want to stay in Harlem no more, I really don't." He was very earnest. He looked at me, then over toward the kitchen window. There was something in his eyes I'd never seen before, some thoughtfulness, some worry all his own. He rubbed the muscle of one arm. "It's time I was getting out of here."

"Where do you want to *go*, Sonny?"

"I want to join the army. Or the navy, I don't care. If I say I'm old enough, they'll believe me."

Then I got mad. It was because I was so scared. "You must be crazy. You goddamn fool, what the hell do you want to go and join the *army* for?"

"I just told you. To get out of Harlem."

"Sonny, you haven't even finished *school*. And if you really want to be a musician, how do you expect to study if you're in the *army*?"

He looked at me, trapped, and in anguish. "There's ways. I might be able to work out some kind of deal. Anyway, I'll have the G.I. Bill when I come out."

"*If* you come out." We stared at each other. "Sonny, please. Be reasonable. I know the setup is far from perfect. But we got to do the best we can."

"I ain't learning nothing in school," he said. "Even when I go." He turned away from me and opened the window and threw his cigarette out into the narrow alley. I watched his back. "At least, I ain't learning nothing you'd want me to learn." He slammed the window so hard I thought the glass would fly out, and turned back to me. "And I'm sick of the stink of these garbage cans!"

"Sonny," I said, "I know how you feel. But if you don't finish school now, you're going to be sorry later that you didn't." I grabbed him by the shoulders. "And you only got another year. It ain't so bad. And I'll come back and I swear I'll help you do *whatever* you want to do. Just try to put up with it till I come back. Will you please do that? For me?"

He didn't answer and he wouldn't look at me.

"Sonny. You hear me?"

He pulled away. "I hear you. But you never hear anything *I* say."

I didn't know what to say to that. He looked out of the window and then back at me. "OK," he said, and sighed. "I'll try."

Then I said, trying to cheer him up a little, "They got a piano at Isabel's. You can practice on it."

And as a matter of fact, it did cheer him up for a minute. "That's right," he said to himself. "I forgot that." His face relaxed a little. But the worry, the thoughtfulness, played on it still, the way shadows play on a face which is staring into the fire.

But I thought I'd never hear the end of that piano. At first, Isabel would write me, saying how nice it was that Sonny was so serious about his music and how, as soon as he came in from school, or wherever he had been when he was supposed to be at school, he went straight to that piano and stayed there until supper-time. And, after supper, he went back to that piano and stayed there until everybody went to bed. He was at the piano all day Saturday and all day Sunday. Then he bought a record player and started playing records. He'd play one record over and over again, all day long sometimes, and he'd improvise along with it on the piano. Or he'd play one section of the record, one chord, one change, one progression, then he'd do it on the piano. Then back to the record. Then back to the piano.

Well, I really don't know how they stood it. Isabel finally confessed that it wasn't like living with a person at all, it was like living with sound. And the sound didn't make any sense to her, didn't make any sense to any of them—naturally. They began, in a way, to be afflicted by this presence that was living in their home. It was as though Sonny were some sort of god, or monster. He moved in an atmosphere which wasn't like theirs at all. They fed him and he ate, he washed himself, he walked in and out of their door; he certainly wasn't nasty or unpleasant or rude, Sonny isn't any of those things; but it was as though he were all wrapped up in some cloud, some fire, some vision all his own; and there wasn't any way to reach him.

At the same time, he wasn't really a man yet, he was still a child, and they had to watch out for him in all kinds of ways. They certainly couldn't throw him out. Neither did they dare to make a great scene about that piano because even they dimly sensed, as I sensed, from so many thousands of miles away, that Sonny was at that piano playing for his life.

But he hadn't been going to school. One day a letter came from the school board and Isabel's mother got it—there had, apparently, been other letters but Sonny had torn them up. This day, when Sonny came in, Isabel's mother showed him the letter and asked where he'd been spending his time. And she finally got it out of him that he'd been down in Greenwich Village, with musicians and other characters, in a white girl's apartment. And this scared her and she started to scream at him and what came up, once she began—though she denies it to this day—was what sacrifices they were making to give Sonny a decent home and how little he appreciated it.

Sonny didn't play the piano that day. By evening, Isabel's mother had calmed down but then there was the old man to deal with, and Isabel herself. Isabel says she did her best to be calm but she broke down and started crying. She says she just watched Sonny's face. She could tell, by watching him, what was happening with him, and what was happening was that they penetrated his cloud, they had reached him. Even if their fingers had been a thousand times more gentle than human fingers ever are, he could hardly help feeling that they had stripped him naked and were spitting on that nakedness. For he also had to see that his presence, that music, which was life or death to him, had been torture for them and that they had endured it, not at all for his sake, but only for mine. And Sonny couldn't take that. He can take it a little better today than he could then but he's still not very good at it and, frankly, I don't know anybody who is.

The silence of the next few days must have been louder than the sound of all the music ever played since time began. One morning, before she went to work, Isabel was in his room for something and she suddenly realized that all of his records were gone. And she knew for certain that he was gone. And he was. He went as far as the navy would carry him. He finally sent me a postcard from some place in Greece and that was the first I knew that Sonny was still alive. I didn't see him any more until we were both back in New York and the war had long been over.

He was a man by then, of course, but I wasn't willing to see it. He came by the house from time to time, but we fought almost every time we met. I didn't like the way he carried himself, loose and dreamlike all the time, and I didn't like his friends, and his music seemed to be merely an excuse for the life he led. It sounded just that weird and disordered.

Then we had a fight, a pretty awful fight, and I didn't see him for months. By and by I looked him up, where he was living, in a furnished room in the Village, and I tried to make it up. But there were lots of people in the room and Sonny just lay on his bed, and he wouldn't come downstairs with me, and he treated these other people as though they were his family and I weren't. So I got mad and then he got mad, and then I told him that he might just as well be dead as live the way he was living. Then he stood up and he told me not to worry about him any more in life, that he *was* dead as far as I was concerned. Then he pushed me to the door and the other people looked on as though nothing were happening, and he slammed the door behind me. I stood in the hallway, staring at the door. I heard somebody laugh in the room and then the tears came to my eyes. I started down the steps, whistling to keep from crying, I kept whistling to myself, *You going to need me, baby, one of these cold, rainy days.*

I read about Sonny's trouble in the spring. Little Grace died in the fall. She was a beautiful little girl. But she only lived a little over two years. She died of polio and she suffered. She had a slight fever for a couple of days, but it didn't seem like anything and we just kept her in bed. And we would certainly have called the doctor, but the fever dropped, she seemed to be all right. So we thought it had just been a cold. Then, one day, she was up, playing, Isabel was in the kitchen fixing lunch for the two boys when they'd come in from school, and she heard Grace fall down in the living room. When you have a lot of children you don't always start running when one of them falls, unless they start screaming or something. And, this time, Grace was quiet. Yet, Isabel says that when she heard that *thump* and then that silence, something happened in her to make her afraid. And she ran to the living room and there was little Grace on the floor, all twisted up, and the reason she hadn't screamed was that she couldn't get her breath. And when she did scream, it was the worst sound, Isabel says, that she'd ever heard in all her life, and she still hears it sometimes in her dreams. Isabel will sometimes wake me up with a low, moaning, strangled sound and I have to be quick to awaken her and hold her to me and where Isabel is weeping against me seems a mortal wound.

I think I may have written Sonny the very day that little Grace was buried. I was sitting in the living room in the dark, by myself, and I suddenly thought of Sonny. My trouble made his real.

One Saturday afternoon, when Sonny had been living with us, or, anyway, been in our house, for nearly two weeks, I found myself wandering aimlessly about the living room, drinking from a can of beer, and trying to work up the courage to search Sonny's room. He was out, he was usually out whenever I was home, and Isabel had taken the children to see their grandparents. Suddenly I was standing still in front of the living room window, watching Seventh Avenue. The idea of searching Sonny's room made me still. I scarcely dared to admit to myself what I'd be searching for. I didn't know what I'd do if I found it. Or if I didn't.

On the sidewalk across from me, near the entrance to a barbecue joint, some people were holding an old-fashioned revival meeting. The barbecue cook, wearing a dirty white apron, his conked hair reddish and metallic in the pale sun, and a cigarette between his lips, stood in the doorway, watching them. Kids and older people paused in their errands and stood there, along with some older men and a couple of very tough-looking women who watched everything that happened on the avenue, as though they owned it, or were maybe owned by it. Well, they were watching this, too. The revival was being carried on by three sisters in black, and a brother. All they had were their voices and their Bibles and a tambourine. The brother was testifying and while he testified two of the sisters stood together, seeming to say, amen, and the third sister walked around with the tambourine outstretched and a couple of people dropped coins into it. Then the brother's testimony ended and the sister who had been taking up the collection dumped the coins into her palm and transferred them to the pocket of her long black robe. Then she raised both hands, striking the tambourine against the air, and then against one hand, and she started to sing. And the two other sisters and the brothers joined in.

It was strange, suddenly, to watch, though I had been seeing these street meetings all my life. So, of course, had everybody else down there. Yet, they paused and watched and listened and I stood still at the window, "*Tis the old ship of Zion,*" they sang, and the sister with the tambourine kept a steady, jangling beat, "*it has rescued many a thousand!"* Not a soul under the sound of their voices was hearing this song for the first time, not one of them had been rescued. Nor had they seen much in the way of rescue work being down around them. Neither did they especially believe in the holiness of the three sisters and the brother, they knew too much about them, knew where they lived, and how. The woman with the tambourine, whose voice dominated the air, whose face was bright with joy, was divided by very little from the woman who stood watching her, a cigarette between her heavy, chapped lips, her hair a cuckoo's nest, her face scarred and swollen from many beatings, and her black eyes glittering like coal. Perhaps they both knew this, which was why, when, as rarely, they addressed each other, they addressed each other as Sister. As the singing filled the air the watching, listening faces underwent a change, the eyes focusing on some-thing within; the music seemed to soothe a poison out of them; and time seemed, nearly, to fall away from the sullen, belligerent, battered faces, as though they were fleeing back to their first condition, while dreaming of their last. The barbecue cook half shook his head and smiled, and dropped his cigarette and disappeared into his joint. A man fumbled in his pockets for change and stood holding it in his hand impatiently, as though he had just remembered a pressing appointment further up the avenue. He looked furious. Then I saw Sonny, standing on the edge of the crowd. He was carrying a wide, flat notebook with a green cover, and it made him look, from where I was standing, almost like a schoolboy. The coppery sun brought out the copper in his skin, he was very faintly smiling, standing very still. Then the sing-ing stopped, the tambourine turned into a collection plate again. The furious man dropped in his coins and vanished, so did a couple of the women, and Sonny dropped some change in the plate, looking directly at the woman with a little smile. He started across the avenue, toward the house. He has a slow, loping walk, something like the way Harlem hipsters walk, only he's imposed on this his own halfbeat. I had never really noticed it before.

I stayed at the window, both relieved and apprehensive. As Sonny disappeared from my sight, they began singing again. And they were still singing when his key turned in the lock.

"Hey," he said.

"Hey, yourself. You want some beer?"

"No. Well, maybe." But he came up to the window and stood beside me, looking out. "What a warm voice," he said.

They were singing *If I could only hear my mother pray again!*

"Yes," I said, "and she can sure beat that tambourine."

"But what a terrible song," he said, and laughed. He dropped his notebook on the sofa and disappeared into the kitchen. "Where's Isabel and the kids?"

"I think they went to see their grandparents. You hungry?"

"No." He came back into the living room with his can of beer. "You want to come some place with me tonight?"

I sensed, I don't know how, that I couldn't possibly say no. "Sure. Where?"

He sat down on the sofa and picked up his notebook and started leafing through it. "I'm going to sit in with some fellows in a joint in the Village."

"You mean, you're going to play, tonight?"

"That's right." He took a swallow of his beer and moved back to the window. He gave me a sidelong look. "If you can stand it."

"I'll try," I said.

He smiled to himself and we both watched as the meeting across the way broke up. The three sisters and the brother, heads bowed, were singing *God be with you till we meet again*. The faces around them were very quiet. Then the song ended. The small crowd dispersed. We watched the three women and the lone man walk slowly up the avenue.

"When she was singing before," said Sonny, abruptly, "her voice reminded me for a minute of what heroin feels like sometimes—when it's in your veins. It makes you feel sort of warm and cool at the same time. And distant. And—and sure." He sipped his beer, very deliberately not looking at me. I watched his face. "It makes you feel—in control. Sometimes you've got to have that feeling."

"Do you?" I sat down slowly in the easy chair.

"Sometimes." He went to the sofa and picked up his notebook again. "Some people do."

"In order," I asked, "to play?" And my voice was very ugly, full of contempt and anger.

"Well"—he looked at me with great, troubled eyes, as though, in fact, he hoped his eyes would tell me things he could never otherwise say—"they *think* so. And *if* they think so—!"

"And what do *you* think?" I asked.

He sat on the sofa and put his can of beer on the floor. "I don't know," he said, and I couldn't be sure if he were answering my question or pursuing his thoughts. His face didn't tell me. "It's not so much to *play*. It's to *stand* it, to be able to make it at all. On any level." He frowned and smiled: "In order to keep from shaking to pieces."

"But these friends of yours," I said, "they seem to shake themselves to pieces pretty goddamn fast."

"Maybe." He played with the notebook. And something told me that I should curb my tongue, that Sonny was doing his best to talk, that I should listen. "But of course you only know the ones that've gone to pieces. Some don't—or at least they haven't *yet* and that's just about all *any* of us can say." He paused. "And then there are some who just live, really, in hell, and they know it and they see what's happening and they go right on. I don't know." He sighed, dropped the notebook, folded his arms. "Some guys, you can tell from the way they play, they on something *all* the time. And you can see that, well, it makes something real for them. But of course," he picked up his beer from the floor and sipped it and put the can down again, "they *want* to, too, you've got to see that. Even some of them that say they don't—*some*, not all."

"And what about you?" I asked—I couldn't help it. "What about you? Do *you* want to?"

He stood up and walked to the window and remained silent for a long time. Then he sighed. "Me," he said. Then: "While I was downstairs before, on my way here, listening to that woman sing, it struck me all of a sudden how much suffering she must have had to go through—to sing like that. It's *repulsive* to think you have to suffer that much."

I said: "But there's no way not to suffer—is there, Sonny?"

"I believe not," he said and smiled, "but that's never stopped anyone from trying." He looked at me. "Has it?" I realized, with this mocking look, that there stood between us, forever, beyond the power of time or forgiveness, the fact that I had held silence—so long!—when he had needed human speech to help him. He turned back to the window. "No, there's no way not to suffer. But you try all kinds of ways to keep from drowning in it, to keep on top of it, and to make it seem well, like *you*. Like you did something, all right, and now you're suffering for it. You know?" I said nothing. "Well you know," he said, impatiently, "why *do* people suffer? Maybe it's better to do something to give it a reason, *any* reason."

"But we just agreed," I said, "that there's no way not to suffer. Isn't it better, then, just to—take it?"

"But nobody just takes it," Sonny cried, "that's what I'm telling you! *Everybody* tries not to. You're just hung up on the *way* some people try—it's not *your* way!"

The hair on my face began to itch, my face felt wet. "That's not true," I said, "that's not true. I don't give a damn what other people do, I don't even care how they suffer. I just care how *you* suffer." And he looked at me. "Please believe me," I said, "I don't want to see you—die—trying not to suffer."

"I won't," he said, flatly, "die trying not to suffer. At least, not any faster than anybody else."

"But there's no need," I said, trying to laugh, "is there? in killing yourself."

I wanted to say more, but I couldn't. I wanted to talk about will power and how life could be—well, beautiful. I wanted to say that it was all within; but was it? or, rather, wasn't that exactly the trouble? And I wanted to promise that I would never fail him again. But it would all have sounded—empty words and lies.

So I made the promise to myself and prayed that I would keep it.

"It's terrible sometimes, inside," he said, "that's what's the trouble. You walk these streets, black and funky and cold, and there's not really a living ass to talk to, and there's nothing shaking, and there's no way of getting it out—that storm inside, You can't talk it and you can't make love with it, and when you finally try to get with it and play it, you realize *nobody's* listening. So *you've* got to listen. You got to find a way to listen."

And then he walked away from the window and sat on the sofa again, as though all the wind had suddenly been knocked out of him. "Sometimes you'll do *anything* to play, even cut your mother's throat." He laughed and looked at me. "Or your brother's." Then he sobered. "Or your own." Then: "Don't worry. I'm all right now and I think I'll *be* all right. But I can't forget—where I've been. I don't mean just the physical place I've been, I mean where I've *been*. And *what* I've been."

"What have you been, Sonny?" I asked.

He smiled—but sat sideways on the sofa, his elbow resting on the back, his fingers playing with his mouth and chin, not looking at me. "I've been something I didn't recognize, didn't know I could be. Didn't know anybody could be." He stopped, looking inward, looking helplessly young, looking old. "I'm not talking about it now because I feel *guilty* or anything like that—maybe it would be better if I did, I don't know. Anyway, I can't really talk about it. Not to you, not to anybody," and now he turned and faced me. "Sometimes, you know, and it was actually when I was most *out* of the world, I felt that I was in it, that I was *with* it, really, and I could play or I didn't really have to *play*, it just came out of me, it was there. And I don't know how I played, thinking about it now, but I know I did awful things, those times, sometimes, to people. Or it wasn't that I *did* anything to them—it was that they weren't real." He picked up the beer can; it was empty; he rolled it between his palms: "And other times—well, I needed a fix, I needed to find a place to lean, I needed to clear a space to *listen*—and I couldn't find it, and I—went crazy, I did terrible things to *me*, I was terrible for me." He began pressing the beer can between his hands, I watched the metal begin to give. It glittered, as he played with it, like a knife, and I was afraid he would cut himself, but I said nothing. "Oh well. I can never tell you. I was all by myself at the bottom of something, stinking and sweating and crying and shaking, and I smelled it, you know? *my* stink, and I thought I'd die if I couldn't get away from it and yet, all the same, I knew that everything I was doing was just locking me in with it. And I didn't know," he paused, still flattening the beer can, "I didn't know, I still *don't* know, something kept telling me that maybe it was good to smell your own stink, but I didn't think that *that* was what I'd been trying to do—and—who can stand it?" and he abruptly dropped the ruined beer can, looking at me with a small, still smile, and then rose, walking to the window as though it were the lodestone rock. I watched his face, he watched the avenue. "I couldn't tell you when Mama died—but the reason I wanted to leave Harlem so bad was to get away from drugs. And then, when I ran away, that's what I was running from—really. When I came back, nothing had changed, *I* hadn't changed, I was just—older." And he stopped, drumming with his fingers on the windowpane. The sun had vanished, soon darkness would fall. I watched his face. "It can come again," he said, almost as though speaking to himself. Then he turned to me. "It can come again," he repeated. "I just want you to know that."

"All right," I said, at last. "So it can come again. All right."

He smiled, but the smile was sorrowful. "I had to try to tell you," he said.

"Yes," I said. "I understand that."

"You're my brother," he said, looking straight at me, and not smiling at all.

"Yes," I repeated, "yes. I understand that."

He turned back to the window, looking out. "All that hatred down there," he said, "all that hatred and misery and love. It's a wonder it doesn't blow the avenue apart."

We went to the only nightclub on a short, dark street, downtown. We squeezed through the narrow, chattering jam-packed bar to the entrance of the big room, where the bandstand was. And we stood there for a moment, for the lights were very dim in this room and we couldn't see. Then, "Hello, boy," said a voice and an enormous black man, much older than Sonny or myself, erupted out of all that atmospheric lighting and put an arm around Sonny's shoulder. "I been sitting right here," he said, "waiting for you."

He had a big voice, too, and heads in the darkness turned toward us.

Sonny grinned and pulled a little away, and said, "Creole, this is my brother. I told you about him."

Creole shook my hand. "I'm glad to meet you, son," he said, and it was clear that he was glad to meet me *there*, for Sonny's sake, and he smiled, "You got a real musician in *your* family," and he took his arm from Sonny's shoulder and slapped him, lightly, affectionately, with the back of his hand.

"Well. Now I've heard it all," said a voice behind us. This was another musician, and a friend of Sonny's, a coal-black, cheerful-looking man, built close to the ground. He immediately began confiding to me, at the top of his lungs, the most terrible things about Sonny, his teeth gleaming like a lighthouse and his laugh coming up out of him like the beginning of an earthquake. And it turned out that everyone at the bar knew Sonny, or almost everyone; some were musicians, working there, or nearby, or not working, some were simply hangers-on, and some were there to hear Sonny play. I was introduced to all of them and they were all very polite to me. Yet, it was clear that, for them, I was only Sonny's brother. Here, I was in Sonny's world. Or, rather: his kingdom. Here, it was not even a question that his veins bore royal blood.

They were going to play soon and Creole installed me, by myself, at a table in a dark corner. Then I watched them, Creole, and the little black man, and Sonny, and the others, while they horsed around, standing just below the bandstand. The light from the bandstand spilled just a little short of them and, watching them laughing and gesturing and moving about, I had the feeling that they, nevertheless, were being most careful not to step into that circle of light too suddenly: that if they moved into the light too suddenly, without thinking, they would perish in flame. Then, while I watched, one of them, the small, black man, moved into the light and crossed the bandstand and started fooling around with his drums. Then—being funny and being, also, extremely ceremonious—Creole took Sonny by the arm and led him to the piano. A woman's voice called Sonny's name and a few hands started clapping. And Sonny, also being funny and being ceremonious, and so touched, I think, that he could have cried, but neither hiding it nor showing it, riding it like a man, grinned, and put both hands to his heart and bowed from the waist.

Creole then went to the bass fiddle and a lean, very bright-skinned brown man jumped up on the bandstand and picked up his horn. So there they were, and the atmosphere on the bandstand and in the room began to change and tighten. Someone stepped up to the microphone and announced them. Then there were all kinds of murmurs. Some people at the bar shushed others. The waitress ran around, frantically getting in the last orders, guys and chicks got closer to each other, and the lights on the bandstand, on the quartet, turned to a kind of indigo. Then they all looked different there. Creole looked about him for the last time, as though he were making certain that all his chickens were in the coop, and then he—jumped and struck the fiddle. And there they were.

All I know about music is that not many people ever really hear it. And even then, on the rare occasions when something opens within, and the music enters, what we mainly hear, or hear corroborated, are personal, private, vanishing evocations. But the man who creates the music is hearing something else, is dealing with the roar rising from the void and imposing order on it as it hits the air. What is evoked in him, then, is of another order, more terrible because it has no words, and triumphant, too, for that same reason. And his triumph, when he triumphs, is ours. I just watched Sonny's face. His face was troubled, he was working hard, but he wasn't with it. And I had the feeling that, in a way, everyone on the bandstand was waiting for him, both waiting for him and pushing him along. But as I began to watch Creole, I realized that it was Creole who held them all back. He had them on a short rein. Up there, keeping the beat with his whole body, wailing on the fiddle, with his eyes half closed, he was listening to everything, but he was listening to Sonny. He was having a dialogue with Sonny. He wanted Sonny to leave the shoreline and strike out for the deep water. He was Sonny's witness that deep water and drowning were not the same thing—he had been there, and he knew. And he wanted Sonny to know. He was waiting for Sonny to do the things on the keys which would let Creole know that Sonny was in the water.

And, while Creole listened, Sonny moved, deep within, exactly like someone in torment. I had never before thought of how awful the relationship must be between the musician and his instrument. He has to fill it, this instrument, with the breath of life, his own. He has to make it do what he wants it to do. And a piano is just a piano. It's made out of so much wood and wires and little hammers and big ones, and ivory. While there's only so much you can do with it, the only way to find this out is to try; to try and make it do everything.

And Sonny hadn't been near a piano for over a year. And he wasn't on much better terms with his life, not the life that stretched before him now. He and the piano stammered, started one way, got scared, stopped, started another way, panicked, marked time, started again; then seemed to have found a direction, panicked again, got stuck. And the face I saw on Sonny I'd never seen before. Everything had been burned out of it, and at the same time, things usually hidden were being burned in, by the fire and fury of the battle which was occurring in him up there.

Yet, watching Creole's face as they neared the end of the first set, I had the feeling that something had happened, something I hadn't heard. Then they finished, there was scattered applause, and then, without an instant's warning, Creole started into something else, it was almost sardonic, it was *Am I Blue*. And, as though he commanded, Sonny began to play. Something began to happen. And Creole let out the reins. The dry, low, black man said something awful on the drums, Creole answered, and the drums talked back. Then the horn insisted, sweet and high, slightly detached perhaps, and Creole listened, commenting now and then, dry, and driving, beautiful and calm and old. Then they all came together again, and Sonny was part of the family again. I could tell this from his face. He seemed to have found, right there beneath his fingers, a damn brand-new piano. It seemed that he couldn't get over it. Then, for awhile, just being happy with Sonny, they seemed to be agreeing with him that brand-new pianos certainly were a gas.

Then Creole stepped forward to remind them that what they were playing was the blues. He hit something in all of them, he hit something in me, myself, and the music tightened and deepened, apprehension began to beat the air. Creole began to tell us what the blues were all about. They were not about anything very new. He and his boys up there were keeping it new, at the risk of ruin, destruction, madness, and death, in order to find new ways to make us listen. For, while the tale of how we suffer, and how we are delighted, and how we may triumph is never new, it always must be heard. There isn't any other tale to tell, it's the only light we've got in all this darkness.

And this tale, according to that face, that body, those strong hands on those strings, has another aspect in every country, and a new depth in every generation. Listen, Creole seemed to be saying, listen. Now these are Sonny's blues. He made the little black man on the drums know it, and the bright, brown man on the horn. Creole wasn't trying any longer to get Sonny in the water. He was wishing him Godspeed. Then he stepped back, very slowly, filling the air with the immense suggestion that Sonny speak for himself.

Then they all gathered around Sonny and Sonny played. Every now and again one of them seemed to say, amen. Sonny's fingers filled the air with life, his life. But that life contained so many others. And Sonny went all the way back, he really began with the spare, flat statement of the opening phrase of the song. Then he began to make it his. It was very beautiful because it wasn't hurried and it was no longer a lament. I seemed to hear with what burning he had made it his, with what burning we had yet to make it ours, how we could cease lamenting. Freedom lurked around us and I understood, at last, that he could help us to be free if we would listen, that he would never be free until we' did. Yet, there was no battle in his face now. I heard what he had gone through, and would continue to go through until he came to rest in earth. He had made it his: that long line, of which we knew only Mama and Daddy. And he was giving it back, as everything must be given back, so that, passing through death, it can live forever. I saw my mother's face again, and felt, for the first time, how the stones of the road she had walked on must have bruised her feet. I saw the moonlit road where my father's brother died. And it brought something else back to me, and carried me past it. I saw my little girl again and felt Isabel's tears again, and I felt my own tears begin to rise. And I was yet aware that this was only a moment, that the world waited outside, as hungry as a tiger, and that trouble stretched above us, longer than the sky.

Then it was over. Creole and Sonny let out their breath, both soaking wet, and grinning. There was a lot of applause and some of it was real. In the dark, the girl came by and I asked her to take drinks to the bandstand. There was a long pause, while they talked up there in the indigo light and after awhile I saw the girl put a Scotch and milk on top of the piano for Sonny. He didn't seem to notice it, but just before they started playing again, he sipped from it and looked toward me, and nodded. Then he put it back on top of the piano. For me, then, as they began to play again, it glowed and shook above my brother's head like the very cup of trembling.

—1948

Malcolm X 1925–1965

Malcolm X was a prominent and controversial leader of the Black Nationalism movement during the Civil Rights struggle of the 1950s and 1960s. After a tumultuous and unhappy youth, Malcolm Little, as he was then known, moved to New York City from Boston. In 1946, he was sent to prison for burglary. While in prison, he joined the Nation of Islam, a political and religious organization, and upon his release he changed his last name to "X," to signify the historical alienation and displacement of African Americans.

Throughout his adult life, Malcolm X was a tireless and fiercely independent promoter of African American rights. In direct contrast to Dr. Martin Luther King, Jr., he doubted that nonviolent resistance was the best way to preserve civil rights. He encouraged

Malcolm X encouraged many African Americans, such as Muhammed Ali, to become Black Muslims and stand up for their rights.

AP Photo

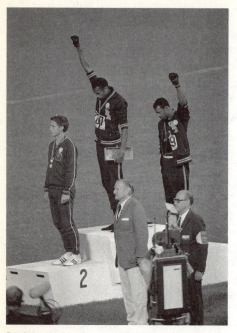

Partly inspired by the principles of Malcolm X, medal winners Tommie Smith and John Carlos give the Black Power salute at the 1968 Olympics awards ceremony
AP Photo

black communities to fight oppression by taking control of their own economic livelihoods. Many of his speeches exhorted listeners to see black nationalism as a "self-help philosophy," a practical attempt to keep local businesses, schools, and governments firmly in the hands of black communities and beyond the influence of Washington, D.C.'s white politicians.

Disillusioned by the rhetoric and hypocrisy of the Nation of Islam, Malcolm founded the Muslim Mosque, Inc., in the spring of 1964. Later, during a trip to Africa, he made the traditional Muslim pilgrimage to Mecca in Saudi Arabia. He returned to the United States a full convert to Sunni Islam and a highly visible figure in political relations between Africa and the United States.

Malcolm X was assassinated while giving a speech in Manhattan on February 21, 1965. *The Autobiography of Malcolm X*, written in collaboration with Alex Haley, is the definitive account of his life, beliefs, and influence.

Further Reading   George Breitman, *Malcolm X Speaks: Selected Speeches and Statements* (1990); Clayborne Carson, *Malcolm X: The FBI File* (1995); Malcolm X, with Alex Haley, *The Autobiography of Malcolm X* (1966).

—*Matthew Ladd, University of Florida*

The Ballot or the Bullet

Mr. Moderator, Brother Lomax,[1] brothers and sisters, friends and enemies: I just can't believe everyone in here is a friend and I don't want to leave anybody out. The question tonight, as I understand it, is "The Negro Revolt, and Where Do We Go From Here?" or "What Next?" In my little humble way of understanding it, it points toward either the ballot or the bullet.

Before we try and explain what is meant by the ballot or the bullet, I would like to clarify something concerning myself. I'm still a Muslim, my religion is still Islam. That's my personal belief. Just as Adam Clayton Powell[2] is a Christian minister who heads the Abyssinian Baptist Church in New York, but at the same time takes part in the political struggles to try and bring about rights to the black people in this country, and Dr. Martin Luther King is a Christian minister down in Atlanta, Georgia,

---

[1] Louis Lomax (1922–1970): Journalist and author who spoke right before Malcolm X.
[2] Adam Clayton Powell, Jr. (1908–1972): Minister and Civil Rights activist, who represented Harlem in the House of Representatives.

who heads another organization fighting for the civil rights of black people in this country; and Rev. Galamison, I guess you've heard of him, is another Christian minister in New York who has been deeply involved in the school boycotts to eliminate segregated education; well, I myself am a minister, not a Christian minister, but a Muslim minister; and I believe in action on all fronts by whatever means necessary.

Although I'm still a Muslim, I'm not here tonight to discuss my religion. I'm not here to try and change your religion. I'm not here to argue or discuss anything that we differ about, because it's time for us to submerge our differences and realize that it is best for us to first see that we have the same problem, a common problem—a problem that will make you catch hell whether you're a Baptist or a Methodist, or a Muslim, or a nationalist. Whether you're educated or illiterate, whether you live on the boulevard or in the alley, you're going to catch hell just like I am. We're all in the same boat and we all are going to catch the same hell from the same man. He just happens to be a white man. All of us have suffered here, in this country, political oppression at the hands of the white man, economic exploitation at the hands of the white man, and social degradation at the hands of the white man.

Now in speaking like this, it doesn't mean that we're anti-white, but it does mean we're anti-exploitation, we're anti-degradation, we're anti-oppression. And if the white man doesn't want us to be anti-him, let him stop oppressing and exploiting and degrading us. Whether we are Christians or Muslims or nationalists or agnostics or atheists, we must first learn to forget our differences. If we have differences, let us differ in the closet; when we come out in front, let us not have anything to argue about until we get finished arguing with the man. If the late President Kennedy could get together with Khrushchev[3] and exchange some wheat, we certainly have more in common with each other than Kennedy and Khrushchev had with each other.

If we don't do something real soon, I think you'll have to agree that we're going to be forced either to use the ballot or the bullet. It's one or the other in 1964. It isn't that time is running out—time has run out! 1964 threatens to be the most explosive year America has ever witnessed. The most explosive year. Why? It's also a political year. It's the year when all of the white politicians will be back in the so-called Negro community jiving you and me for some votes. The year when all of the white political crooks will be right back in your and my community with their false promises, building up our hopes for a letdown, with their trickery and their treachery, with their false promises which they don't intend to keep. As they nourish these dissatisfactions, it can only lead to one thing, an explosion; and now we have the type of black man on the scene in America today—I'm sorry, Brother Lomax—who just doesn't intend to turn the other cheek any longer.

---

[3] **Nikita Khrushchev** (1894–1971): Leader of the Soviet Union after the death of Joseph Stalin.

Don't let anybody tell you anything about the odds are against you. If they draft you, they send you to Korea and make you face 800 million Chinese. If you can be brave over there, you can be brave right here. These odds aren't as great as those odds. And if you fight here, you will at least know what you're fighting for.

I'm not a politician, not even a student of politics; in fact, I'm not a student of much of anything. I'm not a Democrat, I'm not a Republican, and I don't even consider myself an American. If you and I were Americans, there'd be no problem. Those Hunkies that just got off the boat, they're already Americans; Polacks are already Americans; the Italian refugees are already Americans. Everything that came out of Europe, every blue-eyed thing, is already an American. And as long as you and I have been over here, we aren't Americans yet.

Well, I am one who doesn't believe in deluding myself. I'm not going to sit at your table and watch you eat, with nothing on my plate, and call myself a diner. Sitting at the table doesn't make you a diner, unless you eat some of what's on that plate. Being here in America doesn't make you an American. Being born here in America doesn't make you an American. Why, if birth made you American, you wouldn't need any legislation, you wouldn't need any amendments to the Constitution, you wouldn't be faced with civil-rights filibustering in Washington, D.C., right now. They don't have to pass civil-rights legislation to make a Polack an American.

No, I'm not an American. I'm one of the 22 million black people who are the victims of Americanism. One of the 22 million black people who are the victims of democracy, nothing but disguised hypocrisy. So, I'm not standing here speaking to you as an American, or a patriot, or a flag-saluter, or a flag-waver—no, not I. I'm speaking as a victim of this American system. And I see America through the eyes of the victim. I don't see any American dream; I see an American nightmare.

These 22 million victims are waking up. Their eyes are coming open. They're beginning to see what they used to only look at. They're becoming politically mature. They are realizing that there are new political trends from coast to coast. As they see these new political trends, it's possible for them to see that every time there's an election the races are so close that they have to have a recount! They had to recount in Massachusetts to see who was going to be governor, it was so close. It was the same way in Rhode Island, in Minnesota, and in many other parts of the country. And the same with Kennedy[4] and Nixon when they ran for president. It was so close they had to count all over again. Well, what does this mean? It means that when white people are evenly divided, and black people have a bloc of votes of their own, it is left up to them to determine who's going to sit in the White House and who's going to be in the dog house.[4]

---

[4] John F. Kennedy (1917–1963): In the Nixon-Kennedy presidential election of 1960, Kennedy won a majority of votes from urban black voters, tipping the election in his favor.

It was the black man's vote that put the present administration in Washington, D.C. Your vote; your dumb vote, your ignorant vote, your wasted vote put in an administration in Washington, D.C., that has seen fit to pass every kind of legislation imaginable, saving you until last, then filibustering on top of that.[5] And your and my leaders have the audacity to run around clapping their hands and talk about how much progress we're making. And what a good president we have. If he wasn't good in Texas he sure can't be good in Washington, D.C.[6] Because Texas is a lynch state. It is in the same breath as Mississippi, no different; only they lynch you in Texas with a Texas accent and lynch you in Mississippi with a Mississippi accent. And these Negro leaders have the audacity to go and have some coffee in the White House with a Texan, a Southern cracker—that's all he is—and then come out and tell you and me that he's going to be better for us because, since he's from the South, he knows how to deal with the Southerners. What kind of logic is that? Let Eastland[7] be president, he's from the South too. He should be better able to deal with them than Johnson.

In this present administration they have in the House of Representatives 257 Democrats to only 177 Republicans. They control two-thirds of the House vote. Why can't they pass something that will help you and me? In the Senate, there are 67 senators who are of the Democratic Party. Only 33 of them are Republicans. Why, the Democrats have got the government sewed up, and you're the one who sewed it up for them. And what have they given you for it? Four years in office, and just now getting around to some civil-rights legislation. Just now, after everything else is gone, out of the way, they're going to sit down now and play with you all summer long— the same old giant con game that they call filibuster. All those are in cahoots together. Don't you ever think they're not in cahoots together, for the man that is heading the civil-rights filibuster is a man from Georgia named Richard Russell.[8] When Johnson became president, the first man he asked for when he got back to Washington, D.C., was "Dicky"—that's how tight they are. That's his boy, that's his pal, that's his buddy. But they're playing that old con game. One of them makes believe he's for you, and he's got it fixed where the other one is so tight against you, he never has to keep his promise.

So it's time in 1964 to wake up. And when you see them coming up with that kind of conspiracy, let them know your eyes are open. And let them know you got something else that's wide open too. It's got to be the ballot or the bullet. The ballot or the bullet. If you're afraid to use an expression like that, you should get on out of the country, you should get back in the cotton patch, you should get back in the alley. They get all the Negro vote, and after they get it, the Negro gets nothing in

---

[5] … **on top of that:** President Kennedy was slow to initiate Civil Rights reform.

[6] **Texas … D.C.:** President Lyndon Johnson (1908–1973) supported Civil Rights legislation as President, but not as a Texas Senator.

[7] **James Eastland** (1904–1986): Mississippi Senator who argued for racial segregation.

[8] **Richard Russell** (1897–1971): Georgia Senator and vehement segregationist.

return. All they did when they got to Washington was give a few big Negroes big jobs. Those big Negroes didn't need big jobs, they already had jobs. That's camouflage, that's trickery, that's treachery, window dressing. I'm not trying to knock out the Democrats for the Republicans, we'll get to them in a minute. But it is true—you put the Democrats first and Democrats put you last.

Look at it the way it is. What alibis do they use, since they control Congress and the Senate? What alibi do they use when you and I ask, "Well, when are you going to keep your promise?" They blame the Dixiecrats.[9] What is a Dixiecrat? A Democrat. A Dixiecrat is nothing but a Democrat in disguise. The titular head of the Democrats is also the head of the Dixiecrats, because the Dixiecrats are a part of the Democratic Party. The Democrats have never kicked the Dixiecrats out of the party. The Dixiecrats bolted themselves once, but the Democrats didn't put them out. Imagine, these lowdown Southern segregationists put the Northern Democrats down. But the Northern Democrats have never put the Dixiecrats down. No, look at that thing the way it is. They have got a con game going on, a political con game, and you and I are in the middle. It's time for you and me to wake up and start looking at it like it is, and trying to understand it like it is, and then we can deal with it like it is.

The Dixiecrats in Washington, D.C., control the key committees that run the government. The only reason the Dixiecrats control these committees is because they have seniority. The only reason they have seniority is because they come from states where Negroes can't vote. This is not even a government that's based on democracy. It is not a government that is made up of representatives of the people. Half of the people in the South can't even vote. Eastland is not even supposed to be in Washington. Half of the senators and congressmen who occupy these key positions in Washington, D.C., are there illegally, are there unconstitutionally.

I was in Washington, D.C., a week ago Thursday, when they were debating whether or not they should let the bill come onto the floor. And in the back of the room where the Senate meets, there's a huge map of the United States, and on that map it shows the location of Negroes throughout the country. And it shows that the Southern section of the country, the states that are most heavily concentrated with Negroes, are the ones that have senators and congressmen standing up filibustering and doing all other kinds of trickery to keep the Negro from being able to vote. This is pitiful. But it's not pitiful for us any longer; it's actually pitiful for the white man, because soon now, as the Negro awakens a little more and sees the vise that he's in, sees the bag that he's in, sees the real game that he's in, then the Negro's going to develop a new tactic.

These senators and congressmen actually violate the constitutional amendments that guarantee the people of that particular state or country the right to vote.

---

[9] **Dixiecrats:** Racist Southerners who split away from the Democratic Party to support Strom Thurmond's bid for the presidency as a third-party candidate in 1948.

And the Constitution itself has within it the machinery to expel any representative from a state where the voting rights of the people are violated. You don't even need new legislation. Any person in Congress right now, who is there from a state or a district where the voting rights of the people are violated, that particular person should be expelled from Congress. And when you expel him, you've removed one of the obstacles in the path of any real meaningful legislation in this country. In fact, when you expel them, you don't need new legislation, because they will be replaced by black representatives from counties and districts where the black man is in the majority, not in the minority.

If the black man in these Southern states had his full voting rights, the key Dixiecrats in Washington, D.C., which means the key Democrats in Washington, D.C., would lose their seats. The Democratic Party itself would lose its power. It would cease to be powerful as a party. When you see the amount of power that would be lost by the Democratic Party if it were to lose the Dixiecrat wing, or branch, or element, you can see where it's against the interests of the Democrats to give voting rights to Negroes in states where the Democrats have been in complete power and authority ever since the Civil War. You just can't belong to that party without analyzing it.

I say again, I'm not anti-Democrat, I'm not anti-Republican, I'm not anti-anything. I'm just questioning their sincerity, and some of the strategy that they've been using on our people by promising them promises that they don't intend to keep. When you keep the Democrats in power, you're keeping the Dixiecrats in power. I doubt that my good Brother Lomax will deny that. A vote for a Democrat is a vote for a Dixiecrat. That's why, in 1964, it's time now for you and me to become more politically mature and realize what the ballot is for; what we're supposed to get when we cast a ballot; and that if we don't cast a ballot, it's going to end up in a situation where we're going to have to cast a bullet. It's either a ballot or a bullet.

In the North, they do it a different way. They have a system that's known as gerrymandering, whatever that means. It means when Negroes become too heavily concentrated in a certain area, and begin to gain too much political power, the white man comes along and changes the district lines. You may say, "Why do you keep saying white man?" Because it's the white man who does it. I haven't ever seen any Negro changing any lines. They don't let him get near the line. It's the white man who does this. And usually, it's the white man who grins at you the most, and pats you on the back, and is supposed to be your friend. He may be friendly, but he's not your friend.

So, what I'm trying to impress upon you, in essence, is this. You and I in America are faced not with a segregationist conspiracy, we're faced with a government conspiracy. Everyone who's filibustering is a senator—that's the government. Everyone who's finagling in Washington, D.C., is a congressman—that's the government. You don't have anybody putting blocks in your path but people who are a part of the government. The same government that you go abroad to fight for and die for is the government that is in a conspiracy to deprive you of your voting rights, deprive you of your economic opportunities, deprive you of decent housing, deprive you of decent education. You don't need to go to the employer alone, it is the government itself, the government of America, that is responsible for the oppression and exploitation and degradation of black people in this country. And you should drop it in their lap. This government has failed the Negro. This so-called democracy has failed the Negro. And all these white liberals have definitely failed the Negro.

So, where do we go from here? First, we need some friends. We need some new allies. The entire civil-rights struggle needs a new interpretation, a broader interpretation. We need to look at this civil-rights thing from another angle—from the inside as well as from the outside. To those of us whose philosophy is black nationalism, the only way you can get involved in the civil-rights struggle is give it a new interpretation. That old interpretation excluded us. It kept us out. So, we're giving a new interpretation to the civil-rights struggle, an interpretation that will enable us to come into it, take part in it. And these handkerchief-heads who have been dilly-dallying and pussyfooting and compromising—we don't intend to let them pussyfoot and dillydally and compromise any longer.

How can you thank a man for giving you what's already yours? How then can you thank him for giving you only part of what's already yours? You haven't even made progress, if what's being given to you, you should have had already. That's not progress. And I love my Brother Lomax, the way he pointed out we're right back where we were in 1954. We're not even as far up as we were in 1954. We're behind where we were in 1954. There's more segregation now than there was in 1954. There's more racial animosity, more racial hatred, more racial violence today in 1964, than there was in 1954. Where is the progress?

And now you're facing a situation where the young Negro's coming up. They don't want to hear that "turn-the-other-cheek" stuff, no. In Jacksonville, those were teenagers, they were throwing Molotov cocktails.[10] Negroes have never done that before. But it shows you there's a new deal coming in. There's new thinking coming in. There's new strategy coming in. It'll be Molotov cocktails this month, hand grenades next month, and something else next month. It'll be ballots, or it'll be bullets. It'll be liberty, or it will be death. The only difference about this kind of death—it'll be reciprocal. You know what is meant by "reciprocal"? That's one of Brother Lomax's words, I stole it from him. I don't usually deal with those big words because I don't usually deal with big people. I deal with small people. I find you can get a whole lot of small people and whip hell out of a whole lot of big people. They haven't got anything to lose, and they've got everything to gain. And they'll let you know in a minute: "It takes two to tango; when I go, you go."

---

[10] **Molotov cocktail:** Bomb made from a bottle filled with gasoline.

The black nationalists, those whose philosophy is black nationalism, in bringing about this new interpretation of the entire meaning of civil rights, look upon it as meaning, as Brother Lomax has pointed out, equality of opportunity. Well, we're justified in seeking civil rights, if it means equality of opportunity, because all we're doing there is trying to collect for our investment. Our mothers and fathers invested sweat and blood. Three hundred and ten years we worked in this country without a dime in return—I mean without a dime in return. You let the white man walk around here talking about how rich this country is, but you never stop to think how it got rich so quick. It got rich because you made it rich.

You take the people who are in this audience right now. They're poor, we're all poor as individuals. Our weekly salary individually amounts to hardly anything. But if you take the salary of everyone in here collectively it'll fill up a whole lot of baskets. It's a lot of wealth. If you can collect the wages of just these people right here for a year, you'll be rich—richer than rich. When you look at it like that, think how rich Uncle Sam had to become, not with this handful, but millions of black people. Your and my mother and father, who didn't work an eight-hour shift, but worked from "can't see" in the morning until "can't see" at night, and worked for nothing, making the white man rich, making Uncle Sam rich.

This is our investment. This is our contribution—our blood. Not only did we give of our free labor, we gave of our blood. Every time he had a call to arms, we were the first ones in uniform. We died on every battlefield the white man had. We have made a greater sacrifice than anybody who's standing up in America today. We have made a greater contribution and have collected less. Civil rights, for those of us whose philosophy is black nationalism, means: "Give it to us now. Don't wait for next year. Give it to us yesterday, and that's not fast enough."

I might stop right here to point out one thing. Whenever you're going after something that belongs to you, anyone who's depriving you of the right to have it is a criminal. Understand that. Whenever you are going after something that is yours, you are within your legal rights to lay claim to it. And anyone who puts forth any effort to deprive you of that which is yours, is breaking the law, is a criminal. And this was pointed out by the Supreme Court decision. It outlawed segregation.[11] Which means segregation is against the law. Which means a segregationist is breaking the law. A segregationist is a criminal. You can't label him as anything other than that. And when you demonstrate against segregation, the law is on your side. The Supreme Court is on your side.

Now, who is it that opposes you in carrying out the law? The police department itself. With police dogs and clubs. Whenever you demonstrate against segregation, whether it is segregated education, segregated housing, or anything else,

[11] **It outlawed segregation:** Reference to *Brown v. Topeka* Supreme Court decision to outlaw segregation in public schools.

the law is on your side, and anyone who stands in the way is not the law any longer. They are breaking the law, they are not representatives of the law. Any time you demonstrate against segregation and a man has the audacity to put a police dog on you, kill that dog, kill him, I'm telling you, kill that dog. I say it, if they put me in jail tomorrow, kill—that—dog. Then you'll put a stop to it. Now, if these white people in here don't want to see that kind of action, get down and tell the mayor to tell the police department to pull the dogs in. That's all you have to do. If you don't do it, someone else will.

If you don't take this kind of stand, your little children will grow up and look at you and think "shame." If you don't take an uncompromising stand—I don't mean go out and get violent; but at the same time you should never be nonviolent unless you run into some nonviolence. I'm nonviolent with those who are nonviolent with me. But when you drop that violence on me, then you've made me go insane, and I'm not responsible for what I do. And that's the way every Negro should get. Any time you know you're within the law, within your legal rights, within your moral rights, in accord with justice, then die for what you believe in. But don't die alone. Let your dying be reciprocal. This is what is meant by equality. What's good for the goose is good for the gander.

When we begin to get in this area, we need new friends, we need new allies. We need to expand the civil-rights struggle to a higher level—to the level of human rights. Whenever you are in a civil-rights struggle, whether you know it or not, you are confining yourself to the jurisdiction of Uncle Sam. No one from the outside world can speak out in your behalf as long as your struggle is a civil-rights struggle. Civil rights comes within the domestic affairs of this country. All of our African brothers and our Asian brothers and our Latin-American brothers cannot open their mouths and interfere in the domestic affairs of the United States. And as long as it's civil rights, this comes under the jurisdiction of Uncle Sam.

But the United Nations has what's known as the charter of human rights, it has a committee that deals in human rights. You may wonder why all of the atrocities that have been committed in Africa and in Hungary and in Asia and in Latin America are brought before the UN, and the Negro problem is never brought before the UN. This is part of the conspiracy. This old, tricky, blue-eyed liberal who is supposed to be your and my friend, supposed to be in our corner, supposed to be subsidizing our struggle, and supposed to be acting in the capacity of an adviser, never tells you anything about human rights. They keep you wrapped up in civil rights. And you spend so much time barking up the civil-rights tree, you don't even know there's a human rights tree on the same floor.

When you expand the civil-rights struggle to the level of human rights, you can then take the case of the black man in this country before the nations in the UN. You can take it before the General Assembly. You can take Uncle Sam before a world court. But the only level you can do it on is the level of human rights. Civil rights keeps you under his restrictions, under his jurisdiction. Civil rights keeps you in his pocket. Civil rights means you're asking Uncle Sam to treat you right. Human rights are something you were born with. Human rights are your God-given rights. Human rights are the rights that are recognized by all nations of this earth. And any time any one violates your human rights, you can take them to the world court. Uncle Sam's hands are dripping with blood, dripping with the blood of the black man in this country. He's the earth's number-one hypocrite. He has the audacity—yes, he has—imagine him posing as the leader of the free world. The free world!—and you over here singing "We Shall Overcome." Expand the civil-rights struggle to the level of human rights, take it into the United Nations, where our African brothers can throw their weight on our side, where our Asian brothers can throw their weight on our side, where our Latin-American brothers can throw their weight on our side, and where 800 million Chinamen are sitting there waiting to throw their weight on our side.

Let the world know how bloody his hands are. Let the world know the hypocrisy that's practiced over here. Let it be the ballot or the bullet. Let him know that it must be the ballot or the bullet.

When you take your case to Washington, D.C., you're taking it to the criminal who's responsible; it's like running from the wolf to the fox. They're all in cahoots together. They all work political chicanery and make you look like a chump before the eyes of the world. Here you are walking around in America, getting ready to be drafted and sent abroad, like a tin soldier, and when you get over there, people ask you what are you fighting for, and you have to stick your tongue in your cheek. No, take Uncle Sam to court, take him before the world.

By ballot I only mean freedom. Don't you know—I disagree with Lomax on this issue—that the ballot is more important than the dollar? Can I prove it? Yes. Look in the UN. There are poor nations in the UN, yet those poor nations can get together with their voting power and keep the rich nations from making a move. They have one nation—one vote, everyone has an equal vote. And when those brothers from Asia, and Africa and the darker parts of this earth get together, their voting power is sufficient to hold Sam in check. Or Russia in check. Or some other section of the earth in check. So, the ballot is most important.

Right now, in this country, if you and I, 22 million African-Americans—that's what we are—Africans who are in America. You're nothing but Africans. Nothing but Africans. In fact, you'd get farther calling yourself African instead of Negro. Africans don't catch hell. You're the only one catching hell. They don't have to pass civil-rights bills for Africans. An African can go anywhere he wants right now. All you've got to do is tie your head up. That's right, go anywhere you want. Just stop being a Negro. Change your name to Hoogagagooba. That'll show you how silly the white man is. You're dealing with a silly man. A friend of mine who's very dark put a turban on his head and went into a restaurant in Atlanta before they called themselves desegregated. He went into a white restaurant, he sat down, they served him, and he said, "What would happen if a Negro came in here?" And there he's sitting, black as night, but because he had his head wrapped up the waitress looked back at him and says, "Why, there wouldn't no nigger dare come in here."

So, you're dealing with a man whose bias and prejudice are making him lose his mind, his intelligence, every day. He's frightened. He looks around and sees what's taking place on this earth, and he sees that the pendulum of time is swinging in your direction. The dark people are waking up. They're losing their fear of the white man. No place where he's fighting right now is he winning. Everywhere he's fighting, he's fighting someone your and my complexion. And they're beating him. He can't win any more. He's won his last battle. He failed to win the Korean War. He couldn't win it. He had to sign a truce. That's a loss. Any time Uncle Sam, with all his machinery for warfare, is held to a draw by some rice-eaters, he's lost the battle. He had to sign a truce. America's not supposed to sign a truce. She's supposed to be bad. But she's not bad any more. She's bad as long as she can use her hydrogen bomb, but she can't use hers for fear Russia might use hers. Russia can't use hers, for fear that Sam might use his. So, both of them are weaponless. They can't use the weapon because each's weapon nullifies the other's. So the only place where action can take place is on the ground. And the white man can't win another war fighting on the ground. Those days are over. The black man knows it, the brown man knows it, the red man knows it, and the yellow man knows it. So they engage him in guerrilla warfare. That's not his style. You've got to have heart to be a guerrilla warrior, and he hasn't got any heart. I'm telling you now.

I just want to give you a little briefing on guerrilla warfare because, before you know it, before you know it—It takes heart to be a guerrilla warrior because you're on your own. In conventional warfare you have tanks and a whole lot of other people with you to back you up, planes over your head and all that kind of stuff. But a guerrilla is on his own. All you have is a rifle, some sneakers and a bowl of rice, and that's all you need—and a lot of heart. The Japanese on some of those islands in the Pacific, when the American soldiers landed, one Japanese sometimes could hold the whole army off. He'd just wait until the sun went down, and when the sun went down they were all equal. He would take his little blade and slip from bush to bush, and from American to American. The white soldiers couldn't cope with that. Whenever you see a white soldier that fought in the Pacific, he has the shakes, he has a nervous condition, because they scared him to death.

The same thing happened to the French up in French Indochina.[12] People who just a few years previously were rice farmers got together and ran the heavily-mechanized French army out of Indochina. You don't need it—modern warfare today won't work. This is the day of the guerrilla. They did the same thing in Algeria.

---

[12] French Indochina: Old nation that contained modern-day Vietnam, Laos, and Cambodia.

Algerians, who were nothing but Bedouins, took a rifle and sneaked off to the hills, and de Gaulle[13] and all of his highfalutin' war machinery couldn't defeat those guerrillas. Nowhere on this earth does the white man win in a guerrilla warfare. It's not his speed. Just as guerrilla warfare is prevailing in Asia and in parts of Africa and in parts of Latin America, you've got to be mighty naive, or you've got to play the black man cheap, if you don't think some day he's going to wake up and find that it's got to be the ballot or the bullet.

I would like to say, in closing, a few things concerning the Muslim Mosque, Inc., which we established recently in New York City. It's true we're Muslims and our religion is Islam, but we don't mix our religion with our politics and our economics and our social and civil activities—not any more. We keep our religion in our mosque. After our religious services are over, then as Muslims we become involved in political action, economic action and social and civic action. We become involved with anybody, anywhere, any time and in any manner that's designed to eliminate the evils, the political, economic and social evils that are afflicting the people of our community.

The political philosophy of black nationalism means that the black man should control the politics and the politicians in his own community; no more. The black man in the black community has to be re-educated into the science of politics so he will know what politics is supposed to bring him in return. Don't be throwing out any ballots. A ballot is like a bullet. You don't throw your ballots until you see a target, and if that target is not within your reach, keep your ballot in your pocket. The political philosophy of black nationalism is being taught in the Christian church. It's being taught in the NAACP. It's being taught in CORE meetings. It's being taught in SNCC[14] meetings. It's being taught in Muslim meetings. It's being taught where nothing but atheists and agnostics come together. It's being taught everywhere. Black people are fed up with the dillydallying, pussyfooting, compromising approach that we've been using toward getting our freedom. We want freedom *now,* but we're not going to get it saying "We Shall Overcome." We've got to fight until we overcome.

The economic philosophy of black nationalism is pure and simple. It only means that we should control the economy of our community. Why should white people be running all the stores in our community? Why should white people be running the banks of our community? Why should the economy of our community be in the hands of the white man? Why? If a black man can't move his store into a white community, you tell me why a white man should move his store into a black community. The philosophy of black nationalism involves a re-education program in the black community in regards to economics. Our people have to be made to see that any

---

[13] **Charles de Gaulle** (1890–1970): French military leader and statesman.
[14] **NAACP ... CORE ... SNCC:** NAACP, National Association for the Advancement of Colored People; CORE, Congress of Racial Equality; SNCC, Student Nonviolent Coordinating Committee.

time you take your dollar out of your community and spend it in a community where you don't live, the community where you live will get poorer and poorer, and the community where you spend your money will get richer and richer. Then you wonder why where you live is always a ghetto or a slum area. And where you and I are concerned, not only do we lose it when we spend it out of the community, but the white man has got all our stores in the community tied up; so that though we spend it in the community, at sundown the man who runs the store takes it over across town somewhere. He's got us in a vise.

So the economic philosophy of black nationalism means in every church, in every civic organization, in every fraternal order, it's time now for our people to become conscious of the importance of controlling the economy of our community. If we own the stores, if we operate the businesses, if we try and establish some industry in our own community, then we're developing to the position where we are creating employment for our own kind. Once you gain control of the economy of your own community, then you don't have to picket and boycott and beg some cracker downtown for a job in his business.

The social philosophy of black nationalism only means that we have to get together and remove the evils, the vices, alcoholism, drug addiction, and other evils that are destroying the moral fiber of our community. We ourselves have to lift the level of our community, the standard of our community to a higher level, make our own society beautiful so that we will be satisfied in our own social circles and won't be running around here trying to knock our way into a social circle where we're not wanted.

So I say, in spreading a gospel such as black nationalism, it is not designed to make the black man re-evaluate the white man—you know him already—but to make the black man re-evaluate himself. Don't change the white man's mind—you can't change his mind, and that whole thing about appealing to the moral conscience of America—America's conscience is bankrupt. She lost all conscience a long time ago. Uncle Sam has no conscience. They don't know what morals are. They don't try and eliminate an evil because it's evil, or because it's illegal, or because it's immoral; they eliminate it only when it threatens their existence. So you're wasting your time appealing to the moral conscience of a bankrupt man like Uncle Sam. If he had a conscience, he'd straighten this thing out with no more pressure being put upon him. So it is not necessary to change the white man's mind. We have to change our own mind. You can't change his mind about us. We've got to change our own mind about each other. We have to see each other with new eyes. We have to see each other as brothers and sisters. We have to come together with warmth so we can develop unity and harmony that's necessary to get this problem solved ourselves. How can we do this? How can we avoid jealousy? How can we avoid the suspicion and the divisions that exist in the community? I'll tell you how.

I have watched how Billy Graham[15] comes into a city, spreading what he calls the gospel of Christ, which is only white nationalism. That's what he is. Billy Graham is a white nationalist; I'm a black nationalist. But since it's the natural tendency for leaders to be jealous and look upon a powerful figure like Graham with suspicion and envy, how is it possible for him to come into a city and get all the cooperation of the church leaders? Don't think because they're church leaders that they don't have weaknesses that make them envious and jealous—no, everybody's got it. It's not an accident that when they want to choose a cardinal over there in Rome, they get in a closet so you can't hear them cussing and fighting and carrying on.

Billy Graham comes in preaching the gospel of Christ, he evangelizes the gospel, he stirs everybody up, but he never tries to start a church. If he came in trying to start a church, all the churches would be against him. So, he just comes in talking about Christ and tells everybody who gets Christ to go to any church where Christ is; and in this way the church cooperates with him. So we're going to take a page from his book.

Our gospel is black nationalism. We're not trying to threaten the existence of any organization, but we're spreading the gospel of black nationalism. Anywhere there's a church that is also preaching and practicing the gospel of black nationalism, join that church. If the NAACP is preaching and practicing the gospel of black nationalism, join the NAACP. If CORE is spreading and practicing the gospel of black nationalism, join CORE. Join any organization that has a gospel that's for the uplift of the black man. And when you get into it and see them pussyfooting or compromising, pull out of it because that's not black nationalism. We'll find another one.

And in this manner, the organizations will increase in number and in quantity and in quality, and by August, it is then our intention to have a black nationalist convention which will consist of delegates from all over the country who are interested in the political, economic and social philosophy of black nationalism. After these delegates convene, we will hold a seminar, we will hold discussions, we will listen to everyone. We want to hear new ideas and new solutions and new answers. And at that time, if we see fit then to form a black nationalist party, we'll form a black nationalist party. If it's necessary to form a black nationalist army, we'll form a black nationalist army. It'll be the ballot or the bullet. It'll be liberty or it'll be death.

It's time for you and me to stop sitting in this country, letting some cracker senators, Northern crackers and Southern crackers, sit there in Washington, D.C., and come to a conclusion in their mind that you and I are supposed to have civil rights. There's no white man going to tell me anything about my rights. Brothers and sisters, always remember, if it doesn't take senators and congressmen and presidential proclamations to give freedom to the white man, it is not necessary for legislation or

---

[15] **Billy Graham** (b. 1918): World-famous American Protestant evangelist.

proclamation or Supreme Court decisions to give freedom to the black man. You let that white man know, if this is a country of freedom, let it be a country of freedom; and if it's not a country of freedom, change it.

We will work with anybody, anywhere, at any time, who is genuinely interested in tackling the problem head on, nonviolently as long as the enemy is nonviolent, but violent when the enemy gets violent. We'll work with you on the voter registration drive, we'll work with you on rent strikes, we'll work with you on school boycotts—I don't believe in any kind of integration; I'm not even worried about it because I know you're not going to get it anyway; you're not going to get it because you're afraid to die; you've got to be ready to die if you try and force yourself on the white man, because he'll get just as violent as those crackers in Mississippi, right here in Cleveland. But we will still work with you on the school boycotts because we're against a segregated school system. A segregated school system produces children who, when they graduate, graduate with crippled minds. But this does not mean that a school is segregated because it's all black. A segregated school means a school that is controlled by people who have no real interest in it whatsoever.

Let me explain what I mean. A segregated district or community is a community in which people live, but outsiders control the politics and the economy of that community. They never refer to the white section as a segregated community. It's the all-Negro section that's a segregated community. Why? The white man controls his own school, his own bank, his own economy, his own politics, his own everything, his own community—but he also controls yours. When you're under someone else's control, you're segregated. They'll always give you the lowest or the worst that there is to offer, but it doesn't mean you're segregated just because you have your own. You've got to control your own. Just like the white man has control of his, you need to control yours.

You know the best way to get rid of segregation? The white man is more afraid of separation than he is of integration. Segregation means that he puts you away from him, but not far enough for you to be out of his jurisdiction; separation means you're gone. And the white man will integrate faster than he'll let you separate. So we will work with you against the segregated school system because it's criminal, because it is absolutely destructive, in every way imaginable, to the minds of the children who have to be exposed to that type of crippling education.

Last but not least, I must say this concerning the great controversy over rifles and shotguns. The only thing that I've ever said is that in areas where the government has proven itself either unwilling or unable to defend the lives and the property of Negroes, it's time for Negroes to defend themselves. Article number two of the constitutional amendments provides you and me the right to own a rifle or a shotgun. It is constitutionally legal to own a shotgun or a rifle. This doesn't mean you're going to get a rifle and form battalions and go out looking for white folks, although you'd be within your rights—I mean, you'd be justified; but that would be illegal and we don't do anything illegal. If the white man doesn't want the black man buying rifles and shotguns, then let the government do its job. That's all. And don't let the white man come to you and ask you what you think about what Malcolm says—why, you old Uncle Tom. He would never ask you if he thought you were going to say "Amen!" No, he is making a Tom out of you.

So, this doesn't mean forming rifle clubs and going out looking for people, but it is time, in 1964, if you are a man, to let that man know. If he's not going to do his job in running the government and providing you and me with the protection that our taxes are supposed to be for, since he spends all those billions for his defense budget, he certainly can't begrudge you and me spending $12 or $15 for a single-shot, or double-action. I hope you understand. Don't go out shooting people, but any time, brothers and sisters, and especially the men in this audience—some of you wearing Congressional Medals of Honor, with shoulders this wide, chests this big, muscles that big—any time you and I sit around and read where they bomb a church and murder in cold blood, not some grownups, but four little girls while they were praying to the same god the white man taught them to pray to, and you and I see the government go down and can't find who did it.[16]

Why, this man—he can find Eichmann[17] hiding down in Argentina somewhere. Let two or three American soldiers, who are minding somebody else's business way over in South Vietnam, get killed, and he'll send battleships, sticking his nose in their business. He wanted to send troops down to Cuba and make them have what he calls free elections—this old cracker who doesn't have free elections in his own country. No, if you never see me another time in your life, if I die in the morning, I'll die saying one thing: the ballot or the bullet, the ballot or the bullet.

If a Negro in 1964 has to sit around and wait for some cracker senator to filibuster when it comes to the rights of black people, why, you and I should hang our heads in shame. You talk about a march on Washington in 1963, you haven't seen anything. There's some more going down in '64. And this time they're not going like they went last year. They're not going singing "We Shall Overcome." They're not going with white friends. They're not going with placards already painted for them. They're not going with round-trip tickets. They're going with one-way tickets.

And if they don't want that non-nonviolent army going down there, tell them to bring the filibuster to a halt. The black nationalists aren't going to wait. Lyndon B. Johnson is the head of the Democratic Party. If he's for civil rights, let him go into the Senate next week and declare himself. Let him go in there right now and declare himself. Let him go in there and denounce the Southern branch of his party. Let him go in there right now and take a moral stand—right now, not later. Tell

---

[16] **... can't find who did it:** In 1963, a Birmingham church used by Martin Luther King, Jr. to organize Civil Rights activities was bombed; four black girls died in the explosion.
[17] **Adolph Eichmann (1906–1962):** High-ranking Nazi, who organized deportations to death camps, and fled to Argentina where he was captured.

him, don't wait until election time. If he waits too long, brothers and sisters, he will be responsible for letting a condition develop in this country which will create a climate that will bring seeds up out of the ground with vegetation on the end of them looking like something these people never dreamed of. In 1964, it's the ballot or the bullet. Thank you.

—1964

Gwendolyn Brooks 1917–2000

The poetic achievements and honors Gwendolyn Brooks earned during the last half of the twentieth century were exceptional. Among numerous distinctions, she became the first black winner of a Pulitzer Prize (1950 for *Annie Allen*), was named Poet Laureate of Illinois (1968), and was the first black woman to serve as Poetry Consultant to the Library of Congress (1985–1986). Beginning with *A Street in Bronzeville* in 1945, she produced slim poetry volumes of remarkable quality, including *In the Mecca* (1968), *Family Pictures* (1970), and *Winnie* (1988). In addition, she published an important novel, *Maud Martha* (1953), the autobiographies *Report from Part One* (1972) and *Report from Part Two* (1996), and a handful of children's and instructional books. In all genres, Brooks tended toward brevity. She used dexterous—even playful—diction to portray the struggles, foibles, and virtues of average people.

Brooks described her childhood in Chicago as "sparkly." Her formal education ended with a degree from Woodrow Wilson Junior College in 1936, but she believed that a poet's best training came from reading, an activity encouraged by her parents. From an early age she drew inspiration and instruction from Ralph Waldo Emerson, Emily Dickinson, Langston Hughes, and a host of other writers. Considering her dedication to poetry, it is not surprising that she met her husband, Henry Blakely, in a community poetry workshop in 1941.

By the time her most famous poem, "We Real Cool," appeared in *The Bean Eaters* (1960), Brooks was a recognized master of poetic technique, having put her stamp on such traditional forms as the sonnet. At the Second Black Writers' Conference in 1967, however, she found herself chastened by the energy and vision of a younger generation of writers. She was especially struck by their call to abolish "Negro writing" addressed to and evaluated by a white elite. After the conference, she began to advocate "Black writing" that was "written by Blacks, about Blacks, to Blacks." Deeply influenced by the young writers in the Black Arts Movement, she came to see her earlier works as marred by an "integrationist" impulse. Her new poems rarely employed regular forms or meters. During the next two decades, she tried to leave behind such "embroidery" as patterned rhyme and arcane vocabulary. Her goal was to create poetry that was meaningful and immediately enjoyable to blacks on the street, in taverns, or in prisons. At the same time, she left Harper's, her publisher for over twenty years, and cast her lot with black-owned presses.

Brooks was often frustrated in her attempts to forge an appropriate new "Gwendolynian" style. Moreover, she watched with disappointment as the energy of the Black Arts Movement quickly dissipated. She commented sarcastically on the movement of younger black poets to white-owned presses and to styles reminiscent of her earlier phase. Even so, Brooks maintained a fundamental optimism and unwavering commitment to "family," by which she meant black people everywhere. She poured considerable energy into teaching, mentoring, inspiring, and promoting other writers. She created and funded the Poet Laureate Awards for elementary and secondary students, led discussions with neighborhood children, answered numerous letters from aspiring writers, and used her celebrity to draw attention to the work of less famous black writers. Such humane generosity, abundantly reflected in her most memorable poems, is perhaps the most durable poetic legacy of Gwendolyn Brooks.

Brooks's poem "To the Young Who Want to Die" is written as if it were meant to be spoken in a calm voice to someone who is contemplating suicide. The speaker has obviously experienced life's agonies, and advises the young person to remain calm "through pout or pain or peskyness." Just as spring follows winter, good times—or at least some interesting news—will follow hard times. Reject death and depression, the maternal voice counsels, and try to enjoy life.

Further Reading George E. Kent, *A Life of Gwendolyn Brooks* (1990); Haki R. Madhubuti, *Say That the River Turns: The Impact of Gwendolyn Brooks* (1987); Stephen Wright, *On Gwendolyn Brooks: Reliant Contemplation* (1996).

—*Brett Barney, University of Nebraska*

To the Young Who Want to Die

Sit down. Inhale. Exhale.
The gun will wait. The lake will wait.
The tall gall in the small seductive vial
will wait will wait:
will wait a week: will wait through April.
You do not have to die this certain day.
Death will abide, will pamper your postponement.
I assure you death will wait. Death has
a lot of time. Death can
attend to you tomorrow. Or next week. Death is

just down the street; is most obliging neighbor;
can meet you any moment.

You need not die today.
Stay here—through pout or pain or peskyness.
15   Stay here. See what the news is going to be tomorrow.

Graves grow no green that you can use.
Remember, green's your color. You are Spring.

—1986

Rita Dove (b. 1952)

Rita Dove is known for her bold illuminations of historical events and complex portrayal of African American experiences. Dove's critical eye investigates the subtexts of the past, eschewing the obvious while focusing on forgotten events and individuals. With a melodic style many attribute to her background as a musician and singer, Dove's poems reveal the private deeds beneath public events.

Dove was born in Akron, Ohio, the second of four children. Her father, a chemist, and her mother, a homemaker, encouraged their children to read from a young age. After receiving her B.A. summa cum laude from Miami University in Ohio, Dove traveled to Germany on a Fulbright Scholarship. Upon returning to America, Dove entered the University of Iowa where she received her M.F.A. She married writer Fred Viebahn in 1979. Dove began her teaching career at the University of Arizona in 1981, and in 1989 took a position at the University of Virginia.

Dove published her first collection of poems, *The Yellow House on the Corner*, in 1980, and won the Pulitzer Prize in 1987 for *Thomas and Beulah*. She served as the U.S. Poet Laureate from 1993–1995. In addition to poetry, Dove has written plays, short fiction, and a novel entitled *Through the Ivory Gate*. Her twelfth book of poems, *American Smooth*, appeared in 2004.

Dove included "Wingfoot Lake" in *Thomas and Beulah*. The poem explores divisions between blacks and whites, but also between generations in Dove's African American family. Beulah, the grandmother, seems conservative on the issue of Civil Rights, while the younger members of her family are full of political enthusiasm and optimism.

Further Reading   Therese Steffen, *Crossing Color: Transcultural Space and Place in Rita Dove's Poetry, Fiction, and Drama* (2001); Malin Pereira, *Rita Dove's Cosmopolitanism* (2003); Earl G. Ingersoll, *Conversations with Rita Dove* (2003).

—*Jenna Krajeski, The New Yorker*

Wingfoot Lake

(INDEPENDENCE DAY, 1964)

On her 36th birthday, Thomas had shown her
her first swimming pool. It had been
his favorite color, exactly—just
so much of it, the swimmers' white arms jutting
into the chevrons[1] of high society.
She had rolled up her window.
and told him to drive on, fast.

Now this *act of mercy*: four daughters
dragging her to their husbands' company picnic,
white families on one side and them
on the other, unpacking the same
squeeze bottles of Heinz, the same
waxy beef patties and Salem potato chip bags.
So he was dead for the first time
on Fourth of July—ten years ago

had been harder, waiting for something to happen,
and ten years before that, the girls
like young horses eyeing the track.
Last August she stood alone for hours
in front of the T.V. set
as a crow's wing moved slowly through
the white streets of government.[2]
That brave swimming

scared her, like Joanna saying
Mother, we're Afro-Americans now!
What did she know about Africa?
Were there lakes like this one
with a rowboat pushed under the pier?
Or Thomas' Great Mississippi
with its sullen silks? (There was
the Nile but the Nile belonged
to God.) Where she came from
was the past, 12 miles into town
where nobody had locked their back door,

---

[1] **chevrons:** Badges indicating rank.
[2] **the white streets of government:** Reference to the Civil Rights March on Washington, D.C. on August 28, 1963, during which Martin Luther King, Jr. gave his "I Have a Dream" speech.

and Goodyear[3] hadn't begun to dream of a park
under the company symbol, a white foot
sprouting two small wings.

—1986

Sherman Alexie (b. 1966)

Sherman J. Alexie, Jr., is the author of seventeen books that explore contemporary
Native American experiences. Many of his stories and poems offer imaginative de-
pictions of reservation life in Washington State, while others portray urban experiences in Seattle and different locales. He is known for his use of humor to address
issues facing Native American communities today. A skillful performer, he com-
bines stand-up comedy and cultural commentary at his readings. Through collaboration with filmmakers and musicians, he has ensured that his work will reach
wide audiences.

A Spokane/Coeur d'Alene Indian, Alexie was raised in Wellpinit, a small reservation town in Eastern Washington. Until the eighth grade, he attended a tribal
school on the Spokane Indian Reservation. Hoping to receive a better education, he
opted to leave the reservation to attend a distant high school where he was the only
Native American student. He went on to complete an American Studies degree at
Washington State University.

Alexie's writing career began with the publication of several poetry collections,
including *The Business of Fancydancing* (1991) and *I Would Steal Horses* (1993). A
versatile writer, he then published collections of short stories, *The Lone Ranger and
Tonto Fistfight in Heaven* (1993), *The Toughest Indian in the World* (2000), and *Ten
Little Indians* (2003), additional poetry collections, and two novels, *Reservation Blues*
(1995) and *Indian Killer* (1996). He also wrote the screenplays for *Smoke Signals*
(1999), *49?* (2003), and *The Business of Fancydancing* (2003). Currently living in
Seattle, Alexie has received numerous awards that include the O. Henry Prize and
PEN/Hemingway Award.

Further Reading Andrew Dix, "Escape Stories: Narratives and Native Americans in Sherman
Alexie's *The Lone Ranger and Tonto Fistfight in Heaven*," *Yearbook of English Studies* (2001);
Daniel Grassian, *Understanding Sherman Alexie* (2005).

—Kristen Proehl, College of William and Mary

---

[3] **Goodyear:** Goodyear Tire and Rubber Company was founded in Akron, Ohio, in 1898. Thomas—the character
based on Dove's grandfather—worked for Goodyear.

Because My Father Always Said He Was The Only Indian Who Saw Jimi Hendrix Play "The Star-Spangled Banner" at Woodstock[1]

During the sixties, my father was the perfect hippie, since all the hippies were trying to be Indians. Because of that, how could anyone recognize that my father was trying to make a social statement?

But there is evidence, a photograph of my father demonstrating in Spokane, Washington, during the Vietnam war. The photograph made it onto the wire service and was reprinted in newspapers throughout the country. In fact, it was on the cover of *Time*.

In the photograph, my father is dressed in bell-bottoms and flowered shirt, his hair in braids, with red peace symbols splashed across his face like war paint. In his hands my father holds a rifle above his head, captured in that moment just before he proceeded to beat the shit out of the National Guard private lying prone on the ground. A fellow demonstrator holds a sign that is just barely visible over my father's left shoulder. It read MAKE LOVE NOT WAR.

The photographer won a Pulitzer Prize, and editors across the country had a lot of fun creating captions and headlines. I've read many of them collected in my

Sherman Alexie's story remembers Jimi Hendrix's legendary performance at Woodstock.

© *Allan Koss/The Image Works*

---

[1] **Woodstock:** The rock concert on Max Yasgur's farm in upstate New York from August 15–18, 1969, at which the rock star Jimi Hendrix played the national anthem.

father's scrapbook, and my favorite was run in the *Seattle Times*. The caption under the photograph read DEMONSTRATOR GOES TO WAR FOR PEACE. The editors capitalized on my father's Native American identity with other headlines like ONE WARRIOR AGAINST WAR and PEACEFUL GATHERING TURNS INTO NATIVE UPRISING.

Anyway, my father was arrested, charged with attempted murder, which was reduced to assault with a deadly weapon. It was a high-profile case so my father was used as an example. Convicted and sentenced quickly, he spent two years in Walla Walla State Penitentiary.[2] Although his prison sentence effectively kept him out of the war, my father went through a different kind of war behind bars.

"There was Indian gangs and white gangs and black gangs and Mexican gangs," he told me once. "And there was somebody new killed every day. We'd hear about somebody getting it in the shower or wherever and the word would go down the line. Just one word. Just the color of his skin. Red, white, black, or brown. Then we'd chalk it up on the mental scoreboard and wait for the next broadcast."

My father made it through all that, never got into any serious trouble, somehow avoided rape, and got of prison just in time to hitchhike to Woodstock to watch Jimi Hendrix play "The Star-Spangled Banner."

"After all the shit I'd been through," my father said, "I figured Jimi must have known I was there in the crowd to play something like that. It was exactly how I felt."

Twenty years later, my father played his Jimi Hendrix tape until it wore down. Over and over, the house filled with the rockets' red glare and the bombs bursting in air. He'd sit by the stereo with a cooler of beer beside him and cry, laugh, call me over and hold me tight in his arms, his bad breath and body odor covering me like a blanket.

Jimi Hendrix and my father became drinking buddies. Jimi Hendrix waited for my father to come home after a long night of drinking. Here's how the ceremony worked:

1. I would lie awake all night and listen for the sounds of my father's pickup.
2. When I heard my father's pickup, I would run upstairs and throw Jimi's tape into the stereo.
3. Jimi would bend his guitar into the first note of "The Star-Spangled Banner" just as my father walked inside.
4. My father would weep, attempt to hum along with Jimi, and then pass out with his head on the kitchen table.
5. I would fall asleep under the table with my head near my father's feet.
6. We'd dream together until the sun came up.

---

[2] **Walla Walla State Penitentiary:** Officially known as Washington State Penitentiary, the largest penitentiary in the state, where executions take place.

The days after, my father would feel so guilty that he would tell me stories as a means of apology.

"I met your mother at a party in Spokane," my father told me once. "We were the only two Indians at the party. Maybe the only two Indians in the whole town. I thought she was so beautiful. I figured she was the kind of woman who could make buffalo walk on up to her and give up their lives. She wouldn't have needed to hunt. Every time we went walking, birds would follow us around. Hell, tumbleweeds would follow us around."

Somehow my father's memories of my mother grew more beautiful as their relationship became more hostile. By the time the divorce was final, my mother was quite possibly the most beautiful woman who ever lived.

"Your father was always half crazy," my mother told me more than once. "And the other half was on medication."

But she loved him, too, with a ferocity that eventually forced her to leave him. They fought each other with the kind of graceful anger that only love can create. Still, their love was passionate, unpredictable, and selfish. My mother and father would get drunk and leave parties abruptly to go home and make love.

"Don't tell your father I told you this," my mother said. "But there must have been a hundred times he passed out on top of me. We'd be right in the middle of it, he'd say *I love you*, his eyes would roll backwards, and then out went his lights. It sounds strange, I know, but those were good times."

I was conceived during one of those drunken nights, half of me formed by my father's whiskey sperm, the other half formed by my mother's vodka egg. I was born a goofy reservation mixed drink, and my father needed me just as much as he needed every other kind of drink.

One night my father and I were driving home in a near blizzard after a basketball game, listening to the radio. We didn't talk much. One, because my father didn't talk much when he was sober, and two, because Indians don't need to talk to communicate.

"Hello out there, folks, this is Big Bill Baggins, with the late-night classics show on KROC, 97.2 on your FM dial. We have a request from Betty in Tekoa. She wants to hear Jimi Hendrix's version of 'The Star-Spangled Banner' recorded live at Woodstock."

My father smiled, turned the volume up, and we rode down the highway while Jimi led the way like a snowplow. Until that night, I'd always been neutral about Jimi Hendrix. But, in that near-blizzard with my father at the wheel, with the nervous silence caused by the dangerous roads and Jimi's guitar, there seemed to be more to all that music. The reverberation came to mean something, took form and function.

That song made me want to learn to play guitar, not because I wanted to be Jimi Hendrix and not because I thought I'd ever play for anyone. I just wanted to touch the strings, to hold the guitar tight against my body, invent a chord, and come closer to what Jimi knew, to what my father knew.

"You know," I said to my father after the song was over, "my generation of Indian boys ain't ever had no real war to fight. The first Indians had Custer[3] to fight. My great-grandfather had World War I, my grandfather had World War II, you had Vietnam. All I have is video games."

My father laughed for a long time, nearly drove off the road into the snowy fields.

"Shit," he said. "I don't know why you're feeling sorry for yourself because you ain't had to fight a war. You're lucky. Shit, all you had was that damn Desert Storm.[4] Should have called it Dessert Storm because it just made the fat cats get fatter. It was all sugar and whipped cream with a cherry on top. And besides that, you didn't even have to fight it. All you lost during that war was sleep because you stayed up all night watching CNN."

We kept driving through the snow, talked about war and peace.

"That's all there is," my father said. "War and peace with nothing in between. It's always one or the other."

"You sound like a book," I said.

"Yeah, well, that's how it is. Just because it's in a book doesn't make it not true. And besides, why the hell would you want to fight a war for this country? It's been trying to kill Indians since the very beginning. Indians are pretty much born soldiers anyway. Don't need a uniform to prove it."

Those were the kinds of conversations that Jimi Hendrix forced us to have. I guess every song has a special meaning for someone somewhere. Elvis Presley[5] is still showing up in 7-11 stores across the country, even though he's been dead for years, so I figure music just might be the most important thing there is. Music turned my father into a reservation philosopher. Music had powerful medicine.

"I remember the first time your mother and I danced," my father told me once. "We were in this cowboy bar. We were the only real cowboys there despite the fact that we're Indians. We danced to a Hank Williams[6] song. Danced to that real sad one, you know. 'I'm So Lonesome I Could Cry.' Except your mother and I weren't lonesome or crying. We just shuffled along and fell right goddamn down into love."

"Hank Williams and Jimi Hendrix don't have much in common," I said.

"Hell, yes, they do. They knew all about broken hearts," my father said.

"You sound like a bad movie."

---

[3] **General George Custer** (1839–1876): A successful Civil War commander who later fought in the "Indian Wars" before being killed by a group of Sioux/Cheyenne near Little Big Horn River in Montana.

[4] **Desert Storm:** The Persian Gulf War in 1991, in which an international coalition drove Iraq's forces out of Kuwait.

[5] **Elvis Presley** (1935–1977): Popular rock-and-roll singer and actor.

[6] **Hank Williams** (1923–1953): Famous country music singer, songwriter, guitarist.

"Yeah, well, that's how it is. You kids today don't know shit about romance. Don't know shit about music either. Especially you Indian kids. You all have been spoiled by those drums. Been hearing them beat so long, you think that's all you need. Hell, son, even an Indian needs a piano or guitar or saxophone now and again."

My father played in a band in high school. He was the drummer. I guess he'd burned out on those. Now, he was like the universal defender of the guitar.

"I remember when your father would haul that old guitar out and play me songs," my mother said. "He couldn't play all that well but he tried. You could see him thinking about what chord he was going to play next. His eyes got all squeezed up and his face turned all red. He kind of looked that way when he kissed me, too. But don't tell him I said that."

Some nights I lay awake and listened to my parents' lovemaking. I know white people keep it quiet, pretend they don't ever make love. My white friends tell me they can't even imagine their own parents getting it on. I know exactly what it sounds like when my parents are touching each other. It makes up for knowing exactly what they sound like when they're fighting. Plus and minus. Add and subtract. It comes out just about even.

Some nights I would fall asleep to the sounds of my parents' lovemaking. I would dream Jimi Hendrix. I could see my father standing in the front row in the dark at Woodstock as Jimi Hendrix played "The Star-Spangled Banner." My mother was at home with me, both of us waiting for my father to find his way back home to the reservation. It's amazing to realize I was alive, breathing and wetting my bed, when Jimi was alive and breaking guitars.

I dreamed my father dancing with all these skinny hippie women, smoking a few joints, dropping acid, laughing when the rain fell. And it did rain there. I've seen actual news footage. I've seen the documentaries. It rained. People had to share food. People got sick. People got married. People cried all kinds of tears.

But as much as I dream about it, I don't have any clue about what it meant for my father to be the only Indian who saw Jimi Hendrix play at Woodstock. And maybe he wasn't the only Indian there. Most likely there were hundreds but my father thought he was the only one. He told me that a million times when he was drunk and a couple hundred times when he was sober.

"I was there," he said. "You got to remember this was near the end and there weren't as many people as before. Not nearly as many. But I waited it out. I waited for Jimi."

A few years back, my father packed up the family and the three of us drove to Seattle to visit Jimi Hendrix's grave. We had our photograph taken lying down next to the grave. There isn't a gravestone there. Just one of those flat markers.

Jimi was twenty-eight when he died. That's younger than Jesus Christ when he died. Younger than my father as we stood over the grave.

"Only the good die young," my father said.

"No," my mother said. "Only the crazy people choke to death on their own vomit."

"Why you talking about my hero that way?" my father asked.

"Shit," my mother said. "Old Jesse WildShoe choked to death on his own vomit and he ain't anybody's hero."

I stood back and watched my parents argue. I was used to these battles. When an Indian marriage starts to fall apart, it's even more destructive and painful than usual. A hundred years ago, an Indian marriage was broken easily. The woman or man just packed up all their possessions and left the tipi. There were no arguments, no discussions. Now, Indians fight their way to the end, holding onto the last good thing, because our whole lives have to do with survival.

After a while, after too much fighting and too many angry words had been exchanged, my father went out and bought a motorcycle. A big bike. He left the house often to ride that thing for hours, sometimes for days. He even strapped an old cassette player to the gas tank so he could listen to music. With that bike, he learned something new about running away. He stopped talking as much, stopped drinking as much. He didn't do much of anything except ride that bike and listen to music.

Then one night my father wrecked his bike on Devil's Gap Road and ended up in the hospital for two months. He broke both his legs, cracked his ribs, and punctured a lung. He also lacerated his kidney. The doctors said he could have died easily. In fact, they were surprised he made it through surgery, let alone survived those first few hours when he lay on the road, bleeding. But I wasn't surprised. That's how my father was.

And even though my mother didn't want to be married to him anymore and his wreck didn't change her mind about that, she still came to see him every day. She sang Indian tunes under her breath, in time with the hum of the machines hooked into my father. Although my father could barely move, he tapped his finger in rhythm.

When he had the strength to finally sit up and talk, hold conversations, and tell stories, he called for me.

"Victor," he said. "Stick with four wheels."

After he began to recover, my mother stopped visiting as often. She helped him through the worst, though. When he didn't need her anymore, she went back to the life she had created. She traveled to powwows, started to dance again. She was a champion traditional dancer when she was younger.

"I remember your mother when she was the best traditional dancer in the world," my father said. "Everyone wanted to call her sweetheart. But she only danced for me. That's how it was. She told me that every other step was just for me."

"But that's only half of the dance," I said.

"Yeah," my father said. "She was keeping the rest for herself. Nobody can give everything away. It ain't healthy."

"You know," I said, "sometimes you sound like you ain't even real."

"What's real? I ain't interested in what's real. I'm interested in how things should be."

My father's mind always worked that way. If you don't like the things you remember, then all you have to do is change the memories. Instead of remembering the bad things, remember what happened immediately before. That's what I learned from my father. For me, I remember how good the first drink of that Diet Pepsi tasted instead of how my mouth felt when I swallowed a wasp with the second drink.

Because of all that, my father always remembered the second before my mother left him for good and took me with her. No. I remembered the second before my father left my mother and me. No. My mother remembered the second before my father left her to finish raising me all by herself.

But however memory actually worked, it was my father who climbed on his motorcycle, waved to me as I stood in the window, and rode away. He lived in Seattle, San Francisco, Los Angeles, before he finally ended up in Phoenix. For a while, I got postcards nearly every week. Then it was once a month. Then it was on Christmas and my birthday.

On a reservation, Indian men who abandon their children are treated worse than white fathers who do the same thing. It's because white men have been doing that forever and Indian men have just learned how. That's how assimilation can work.

My mother did her best to explain it all to me, although I understood most of what happened.

"Was it because of Jimi Hendrix?" I asked her.

"Part of it, yeah," she said. "This might be the only marriage broken up by a dead guitar player."

"There's a first time for everything, enit?"

"I guess. Your father just likes being alone more than he likes being with other people. Even me and you."

Sometimes I caught my mother digging through old photo albums or staring at the wall or out the window. She'd get that look on her face that I knew meant she missed my father. Not enough to want him back. She missed him just enough for it to hurt.

On those nights I missed him most I listened to music. Not always Jimi Hendrix. Usually I listened to the blues. Robert Johnson[7] mostly. The first time I heard Robert Johnson sing I knew he understood what it meant to be Indian on the edge of the twenty-first century, even if he was black at the beginning of the twentieth. That

---

[7] **Robert Johnson** (1911–1938): Famous Delta Blues musician, sometimes called "the grandfather of rock-and-roll."

must have been how my father felt when he heard Jimi Hendrix. When he stood there in the rain at Woodstock.

Then on the night I missed my father most, when I lay in bed and cried, with that photograph of him beating that National Guard private in my hands, I imagined his motorcycle pulling up outside. I knew I was dreaming it all but I let it be real for a moment.

"Victor," my father yelled. "Let's go for a ride."

"I'll be right down. I need to get my coat on."

I rushed around the house, pulled my shoes and socks on, struggled into my coat, and ran outside to find an empty driveway. It was so quiet, a reservation kind of quiet, where you can hear somebody drinking whiskey on the rocks three miles away. I stood on the porch and waited until my mother came outside.

"Come on back inside," she said. "It's cold."

"No," I said. "I know he's coming back tonight."

My mother didn't say anything. She just wrapped me in her favorite quilt and went back to sleep. I stood on the porch all night long and imagined I heard motorcycles and guitars, until the sun rose so bright that I knew it was time to go back inside to my mother. She made breakfast for both of us and we ate until we were full.

—1993

Amy Tan (b. 1952)

Amy Tan is one of the most prominent writers in the growing field of contemporary Asian American literature. Having received both popular and academic acclaim, Tan is best known for the way she re-examines immigrant histories and constructions of American culture. Through various narrative devices such as flashbacks and the blurring of myth and reality, Tan investigates the bicultural heritage of Asian Americans and the struggles between first and second generations, particularly those between mothers and daughters. Alienation, animosity, and miscommunication in these relationships are common in her work.

Amy Tan was born in Oakland, California. Her parents emigrated from China in the late 1940s. When Tan was a teenager, both her father and her older brother died from brain tumors. Later, Tan's mother moved her and her younger brother to Switzerland, where she attended high school. At eight, she wrote an essay about a public library that was published in the local newspaper.

Despite her mother's hope that she would become a doctor, Tan's passion for writing remained strong as she attended eight different colleges. She received her B.A.

in English and her M.A. in Linguistics from San Jose State University. She has held a variety of jobs ranging from bartending to counseling handicapped children. Her novels continue to garner widespread critical acclaim and to enjoy long periods on bestseller lists.

Further Reading Bella Adams, *Amy Tan* (2005); Mary Ellen Snodgrass, *Amy Tan: A Literary Companion* (2004).

—*Hilary J. Marcus, College of William and Mary*

Alien Relative

I was there at San Francisco Airport when Helen arrived in this country from Formosa.[1] That was in 1956, maybe sooner than that. In any case, back then she was called Hulan, "Lake Mist." She said her mother named her that because she came into this world like the Queen of Clouds rising from the water at dawn. But I think Helen just made that up. I think probably her mother called her that because she was born already crying a lake of tears.

As I was saying, I was there at the airport with my husband and children, waiting for Hulan to come, this woman I call sister, although she is no such thing. I just said that for the Immigration officials, so I could sponsor her—also because I owed Hulan a debt I had to repay. She helped me leave my first marriage, that time I was married to a bad man. Actually, she did not really help help, only promised not to interfere. In China, that was almost like helping. As for myself, I really did help Hulan. I helped her come to this country. In America, that meant I had to interfere.

"Hey!" I called when I saw Hulan come out of the Customs swinging door, her face bouncing up and down in the crowd. And just like her name, she had mist in her eyes, crying so hard she couldn't see us. It was seven years since the last time I saw her, but she looked as if it had been twice as long, she was so old. Her hair was unstylish, same as always, only now it was hanging down just like a washerwoman's, no curly parts to frame her round face. And she wore an ugly fur coat, the skins bent all stiff to pieces, like an old dead dog dried out on the road. So of course I didn't recognize it, my mink coat, I mean, the same one I loaned her in Shanghai[2] last time I saw her, when I was still dreaming I could buy ten just like it in my rich new American home. Oh, I was mad when I found out later that her ruined coat was mine!

But, as I was saying, that day at the airport, at the Customs door, our whole family was happy to welcome her—her husband and her children, too. I was standing on my tiptoes, holding my young daughter's hand. Actually, I squeezed Pearl's hand too hard. I didn't mean to, of course, but then, with so much waiting and excitement,

---

[1] **Formosa:** The island off the coast of China often called Taiwan.
[2] **Shanghai:** China's largest city, situated on the east coast where the Yangtze River meets the ocean.

and then to finally see Hulan, my old friend who knew all the troubles of my life—well, how did I know what I had done until Pearl screamed, "Let me go, Mommy, let me go!" In front of all those people, she said that. All my life, it seems, Pearl's been saying the same thing. Let me go.

Anyway, we were there, only a few faces away, and still Hulan couldn't see us. Of course she couldn't—she didn't have her glasses on. So my husband, Johnny, lifted our four-year-old son high in the air to call Hulan's attention our way. And little Samuel shouted, "Whoa, horsey! Whoa!" and waved three cowboy hats, two white, one black, two for boys, one for girl, because that's how many children Hulan had. Finally Hulan saw us, and cried back, "Brother! Sister!" I think she called us that just in case the Immigration officials were watching.

She pushed her way through the crowd. Her husband, Henry, came next, just like a person still dream-walking, not believing he was really here. He was holding the baby, Bao-bao Roger. Then came Ming-fei Mary, so small for eight years old … then two suitcases … one box … no more.

Right away I noticed: Only two children, why not three? Where was their middle child, the son who was six years old?

"Feng-yi Frank, where is he?" I asked, still looking.

"Oh, he is coming," Hulan answered slowly, "only later."

Johnny and I looked behind her, thinking she meant one minute later. Then one minute later, when we were still waiting and looking, Henry finally explained it this way: "The money you sent for five tickets, later it was enough for only four."

And still we didn't understand, until Hulan began to cry in a scared way. "You already did so much. How could we ask for more?" Then Henry sat down on a suitcase and covered his face. And Ming-fei Mary started wailing. And little Bao-bao saw all this, turned his mouth down, and cried loud, too.

So that's how we found out: They left Feng-yi behind. Too polite to ask for more money! Too polite to let their middle son come to America! Oh, isn't that the Chinese way—to make all that pain seem like just a small inconvenience?

That day at the airport I can never forget. We were all standing together at last, so many happy people rushing by us. My heart hurt, filled with Hulan's troubles, my stomach ached, mixed with my own anger. I wanted to shout at Hulan, "So stupid! So stupid!" Because I was remembering how much we too had suffered. How Johnny worked overtime, one-dollar-eighty-five for an hour, stacking boxes weekends and nights. How I always bought the fatty pork, twenty cents' saving here and there. How I scolded Pearl so hard for one sock missing, until she shouted, "Leave me alone," and I left her with a big slap mark on her face instead. All those sacrifices to bring so much unhappiness to America!

Of course, we tried to send for Feng-yi right away, as soon as we had more money. But then we found out: no applications for nephews, ten-years waiting list for sons, but first you must be a citizen, no breaking the rules. So, it was seven years more before Hulan and Henry received their citizenship papers, four years more before they were brave enough to tell the authorities, "We have another son." Eleven years altogether before they finally got Feng-yi Frank back. And telling it this way, I make it sound simple.

Anyway, that was long time ago, more than twenty years gone by, all those troubles now forgotten. Today Hulan's an American. Now days she calls herself Helen. Now she thinks life is so easy, doing everything the American way. Like what she said yesterday. I was complaining about my daughter, Pearl, how she never comes to visit, how she never tells me anything over the phone, just, "Oh, Mom, we're fine, don't worry."

And Helen said, "You want her to visit you more often, it's easy. You invite her to your house. That's the American way. These days, kids don't drop in, drop out. You have to ask. Come on this date, such-and-such a time. Like an appointment, see, easy to make."

And I wanted to tell Helen: Easy? You don't remember? It's not so easy to claim back your child.

I was with her, standing in long lines at the Department of Justice. You think Hulan could speak up for herself, a mother who left her son behind? So I came along to use the American rules to push us through first one line then another, one place to get forms, one place to ask questions.

Finally we found the right line, but the woman authority acted like she was too busy stamping official documents—toong! toong!—oh yes, what she was doing was more important than us. Helen pushed forward the application, the one that said, "Petition for Alien Relative." I whispered to Helen from behind, "Talk, talk, tell her your situation."

"I came to this country," Helen began, "but forgot my son."

"Forgot?" the woman said, still stamping, not even looking up. "How can you forget a son?"

"No, no! I can never forget my son," Hulan said, leaning back, scared. "This is not what I meant." The woman authority now looked at Hulan. Hulan looked at me. And I knew what she wanted to say, all those things she told me at her kitchen table these past eleven years. So I stepped to the counter and I told the Immigration authority how this could happen, how you can lose a child, and really, this was nobody's fault.

They were sitting in a courtyard in Formosa, Henry and Hulan, when our telegram came. They took it inside their room, so the neighbors could not see, these strangers who envied you if you had even one grain of rice more. But already, people were whispering, "Overseas! They got a telegram from overseas!"

Hulan dried their hands, it was so steamy hot that day. Then carefully, so carefully, she used a small knife to cut open the envelope and read our one-page message, the words we tried to say clearly, so there would be no delay: "The Red Cross, the church sponsor, all of us are saying to come now, come through. There is an opening. The money is being wired to you."

They walked out of their room, into the courtyard. They looked at their neighbors, who were by their doors watching. Hulan had waited for the day she could do this. "Soon this room will be available," she announced, just like a victor. "We are moving to America!"

Then came the first problem. Their daughter had a TB[3] test, and it said maybe the TB was active, maybe not. In any case, Ming-fei Mary couldn't leave. So they gave an official some of their plane ticket money to say it was not, and later it really turned out it was not. "But in those days," Helen argued with me later, "who knew which way things would go for you without paying a price?"

Now they had only enough money to buy four plane tickets. They didn't think ahead that this would happen, that's how it is when you are scared. So Henry said, "We should write to Winnie and Johnny, ask them for more money."

But Hulan said, "They will think we were careless! Besides, too much time will be wasted before they can answer us yes or no." Because they both knew: In Formosa, wait too long and you can lose your chance forever. Just that day, they had heard it on the radio: at a black-market booth, hundreds of people had pushed and shoved, shouted and fought—then fourteen people were hurt, two people crushed—over one special visa to America, which turned out to be illegal.

For two days and two nights, they argued and cried, deciding what to do. Hulan even tried to sell the mink coat, the same one I gave her before I left China. But then the pawnshop man told Hulan the coat was dirty, trying to bargain her down. So Hulan washed that mink coat with soap and water, washed it until there was nothing left to sell. After that, Henry decided what to do.

"I will stay," he said. "You and the children, you go first." He was once a military official. He knew how to be brave like that, ordering his family to a second-place victory.

But Hulan scolded him bitterly, "What good is a family in America with no father to feed them? I will stay."

Then Henry shouted, "Crazy woman! No mother to guide her children to the right opportunities? You want them to become wild Americans? We are all staying then."

That evening they felt too sick to eat. They lay wide awake on their bed, grieving silently over the opportunity they could no longer use. Then they looked at their

---

[3] TB: Tuberculosis.

three sleeping children, crowded on another bed in the same room, two boys, one girl, growing bigger every day. I have done the same with my own children, so I know. And seeing this, all their anger turned to grief. Because at that moment, as with every moment, neighbors were arguing: "That's my pot! Who said you can use it to cook your smelly food!" Then more people were shouting, "Your food stinks worse!" Every day they heard this, the cursing and shouting, accusing and pleading. They were listening to all this hopelessness coming from rooms filled with people who had once been so rich and powerful in different parts of China, and were now the same kind of poor in one courtyard in Formosa.

In the middle of the night, when the courtyard was finally quiet, Hulan and Henry rose from the bed and went outside. They sat on the ground, looked at the sky, but not at each other.

Hulan spoke first: "Ming-fei's health, it's always been poor."

Then Henry said, "And little Bao-bao—so helpless! Only one year old."

After that they were silent for a long time. The night was black, no stars, no moon. They heard no crickets, felt no cooling wind. Finally Hulan spoke in a trembly voice.

"Yesterday afternoon I saw Feng-yi holding a cocoon in his hand. Just like this, so softly. He was blowing his breath on it, thinking this would make the butterfly pop out and play."

"Six years old, and already so clever," said Henry.

"So patient, so playful," Hulan said, now starting to cry.

"Strong," said Henry, then more loudly, "and obedient, too."

"Our favorite," Hulan whispered in a hoarse voice, "and he knows this, too. Old enough to never forget us."

That morning, Hulan grasped her middle child to her heart and promised him, "I will never forget you, never lose you." And Feng-yi smiled, not knowing what she meant.

In the evening, they took Feng-yi to visit his grandmother. Actually, she was not the real grandmother but a bondservant who married Henry's father after the real grandmother died. In any case, the old lady was glad to take in the little boy. Although, after she put the boy to bed, she scolded Hulan and Henry: "Leaving China was bad enough. Now you're going to America, where it is even worse. What will become of us Chinese people?" They went to the airport that night, when Feng-yi was already dreaming.

On the airplane, they practiced everything about the new country in their minds. They imagined a large Immigration official greeting them with pale eyes and a sly mouth, smiling and encouraging them, "Say anything. In our country, you are free to say anything. Do you love our government?"

"Yes," they practiced saying in English. "We love America, very, very much, more than China, more than Formosa."

And then they imagined this pale-eyed man asking them more questions, trickier ones: "Then where is your other son, the one on this document? Why did you leave him behind? Is he a Communist spy?"

"Oh no, not a spy, just a little boy. He loves America, too."

"Then why didn't you bring him?"

"He was sick, too sick to come."

"I see, and the rest of you, did you bring this same sickness here?"

"Actually he is not sick, nobody is. It's just that we didn't have the money to bring him. This is the truth, only that reason, no money."

"What! You came to our country with not enough money? You came here to beg? Police! Police!"

Before they landed, the visa papers with their names had one name crossed out. I always thought that was a bad-luck thing to do, crossing Feng-yi's name out, like wishing he would be banished from the world—which, of course, is what happened four months later.

I read the letter in Hulan's kitchen. That grandmother, who was not even the real grandmother, wrote to say she was returning to China. "Fukkien[4] food is bad for the stomach," she wrote. "I would rather die in Shanghai than live in Formosa. No more running away. We are going home, Feng-yi and I."

"Henry did this!" cried Hulan. "I insisted I should be the one to stay, Feng-yi should go. Now look what's happened!"

"I said we all should stay," Henry shouted back. "But you! You were dreaming of American cars, a car we could drive back to Formosa to fetch Feng-yi back!"

Day after day, year after year, we heard them arguing like that. I used to sit in Hulan's kitchen. So many times I had to watch the steam rise from her cook pot, the mist clouding her eyes, while she whispered to me—every birthday, every festival day, every time I brought my same-age daughter to her house—how she would never forget him.

Let me tell you, that little boy, Feng-yi, none of us could forget him. For so many years we could not see him. We could not hear him. We could not write to him. He was just a little boy, living in Red China, cut off from the world. But I remember, it was just like he was living in Hulan's kitchen all those years, shouting back, as powerful as any angry ghost.

"My sister, she only forgot to claim her son on the paper," I explained to the Immigration authority. "Now do you understand?"

The authority was not smiling. She said, "Then here's what you should do."

For her forgetfulness, Hulan and Henry had to hire an expensive immigration lawyer. The lawyer they found in the Yellow Pages was Chinese but born in this

---

[4] Fukkien: Province in southern China.

country. Hulan didn't listen when I told her, "A Chinese name doesn't mean Chinese thinking."

Sure enough, this lawyer said—in English—that we needed proof, "a birth certificate," to show this Alien Relative on the application paper had a true relationship with his mother.

"In China," I told the lawyer carefully, "you don't need a certificate to be born. See, when a baby is born, if he is crying, this is proof he is born live. If a woman sacrifices her own breast to feed him, this is proof she is his mother. Okay?"

"What you need," the lawyer said to Hulan, "is an affidavit witnessed by a notary public, signed by witnesses who knew you in China when your son was born."

Hulan shook her head quickly and said, "All those people are dead." But what she really meant was, "All those people are scared to death." Who would be willing to sign an official document when they had their own problems to hide? Maybe they were renting a room for two, when they really had eight or ten people living inside. Maybe they told the officials they were working one job, nine-to-five, but it was really three jobs—graveyard, overtime, weekends—and who knew if all that extra work was illegal to do. In any case, why should anyone lift a hand to help only to have it chopped off?

"Chinese people always help each other out," said the lawyer.

Lucky for Hulan, I remembered Old Auntie Du, her aunt married to her father's brother from long time ago. And this old aunt, over seventy years old, knew she would die soon anyway.

"They can kick me out of this country, okay!" laughed Auntie Du. "Send me back to China, doesn't matter. Anyway, I want to be buried there."

Old Auntie Du signed the affidavit, and she told the notary public several times, "I was right there. These two eyes, these two hands—right there inspecting the cord that tied mother to son, son to mother. Write that down."

Six months later, Feng-yi Frank, the Alien Relative on the petition, arrived at the airport. We were there, at the Customs swinging door, same as in 1956, only now it was 1967. Henry brought his never-forgotten son a cowboy hat. Samuel and Pearl brought their new cousin Silly Putty and a water pistol. And Hulan, I remember, she brought her dreams. Her face had two dark spots under her eyes, two hungry hollows in her cheeks. So many nights of dreaming awake!

I saw how her eyes grew big with hope, staring at each little boy who walked through the Customs door. Her feet were ready to run toward this one—then that one—here, no, over there!

I was the first to know it was Feng-yi Frank standing in front of us. And Hulan was right, when she left her son, he was old enough never to forget. He stared right at his mother, nobody else. That's when Helen's eyes looked up, turned scared, searching for her memory.

His smooth, plump chin, the one she used to lift to her face to kiss, now it pointed down at her, rough and bony hard. His soft little hands, the ones that reached up to her, demanding to be held, now they held tight onto two boxes tied with string, and he didn't even put them down when Hulan hugged him American-style.

But his eyes—they had changed the most, she whispered to me later. Not curious, not eager, never looking back or farther ahead. He seemed to see only what was in front of him, and he showed no opinion in his eyes about any of it. That son, already seventeen years old when he arrived, never let his mother forget what she had done.

Maybe I should have felt more sorry for Hulan. But then I thought, She never told Feng-yi she was sorry. I heard what she said: how Formosa, then America, then China were the reasons for the long delay. "How could I fight three countries?" she told him at the beginning. Later, she bragged about all her hardships to bring him over: "Lawyers, money, affidavit—more complicated than you think!"

Now Feng-yi is an American, life is so easy. He tells everyone to call him Frank. He is almost forty, same as my daughter, Pearl. He lives with his mother and father. Lucky he still has a living father, not like my children. Every evening he has dinner at home, so polite, saying thank you, no thanks when his mother says, "Eat more, eat more!" At night he goes to his job as a security guard, signing people in, signing people out. And when he gets up late in the afternoon, he smokes too many cigarettes, or plays video games on his TV set, or lies underneath an old greasy car and sings to its stomach, "How much is that doggie in the window, the one with the waggle-ly tail."

An American lady from our church once asked Frank, "What was it like living in China, aren't you so glad to be here?" And Frank said, "China wasn't too bad, just boring, same old clothes, nothing to do. Oh, and they didn't let you have pets."

Helen then told that church lady how much Frank always wanted a dog. And that's what he got, a fancy poodle dog, for his twenty-fifth birthday. Puffy head, puffy tail. I tell you this, though, that dog, all those years, lived outside on a cold little porch, because Helen didn't want it to messy up her house. And I saw that dog every time I went to visit—I saw it through the sliding glass door. It was matted and dirty, so skinny, shaking and dancing in a circle every time he saw Frank come home. But Frank didn't even look at that doggie in the window. Although sometimes he still sang that same song, the one with the waggle-ly tail.

I heard Helen complain only one time, about her son, I mean. We were watching Frank, and Frank was watching cars race round and round on the TV set. He sat up, he sat back, he shook his fist and shouted, "Go, you sonabitch, go!" That's when Helen whispered to me, "Look what the Communists did to my son."

I still see Helen almost every day. But she doesn't tell me her troubles. She doesn't cry in her kitchen. She doesn't take my advice anymore. Now she thinks she's giving me advice, helping me. Like the other day. We were sitting in her kitchen, near the sliding glass door. I was watching her dog lying outside, so sad. She was telling me how I should call Pearl.

"Make her some Chinese dumplings," Helen said. "Invite her to come eat. She eats your food, she's just like your little girl again, thanking her mommy."

I pretended not to listen. What does she know? Why should I let her interfere? So instead I told her, "That poodle dog looks sick, real bad."

And she said, "Oh, that dog's okay. It's just old."

The next day that dog died. I was in Helen's kitchen a few days after it happened. I didn't say anything about the dog that was no longer there. I didn't tell Helen how I made the dumplings, how Pearl didn't come. We were just sitting and drinking tea, same as always. Then Helen started to scratch her ankles, then her legs, until she cried out, "Why are those fleas still pinching me? That dog's already dead!"

And I didn't explain to her, because I know how Helen has become. She doesn't understand, not anymore, how something can still hurt you after it's gone.

—1992

Richard Rodriguez (b. 1944)

Richard Rodriguez is an award-winning essayist whose autobiographical writings arise from his experiences as a child growing up in a Hispanic working-class family in California. His opposition to both affirmative action and bilingual education has been controversial, while his exploration of the paradoxes of language, religion, race, class, nationality, and sexuality has secured his reputation as a provocative and engaging author.

Born in San Francisco to Mexican immigrant parents, Rodriguez spent his early years communicating with his family almost exclusively in Spanish. His struggle with his Hispanic heritage began when he entered Catholic parochial school in Sacramento where English was the only language spoken. The challenge to learn English and assimilate into American society inspired his early works. Rodriguez graduated from Stanford, received his M.A. from Columbia, and now lives in San Francisco.

Rodriguez addressed the issues of bilingualism, race, and class in his autobiography *Hunger of Memory: The Education of Richard Rodriguez* (1982). Ten years later, his book *Days of Obligation: An Argument with My Mexican Father* was a runner-up for the 1993 Pulitzer Prize in nonfiction. His third book, *Brown: The Last Discovery of America*, was published a decade later. He has reported and written essays for *The News Hour* with Jim Lehrer. For his essays, he won a George Peabody Award in 1997. He is an editor at the Pacific News Service and contributing editor at *Harper's Magazine*, *U.S. News & World Report*, and the *Los Angeles Times*.

Further Reading Scott London, "A View from the Melting Pot: An Interview with Richard Rodriguez," <http://www.scottlondon.com>; Kevin McNamara, "A Finer Grain: Richard Rodriguez's *Days of Obligation*," *Arizona Quarterly* (1997).

—*Pauline Pauley, formerly of Hollins University*

From Aria[1]: A Memoir of a Bilingual Childhood

I remember, to start with, that day in Sacramento, in a California now nearly thirty years past, when I first entered a classroom—able to understand about fifty stray English words. The third of four children, I had been preceded by my older brother and sister to a neighborhood Roman Catholic school. But neither of them had revealed very much about their classroom experiences. They left each morning and returned each afternoon, always together, speaking Spanish as they climbed the five steps to the porch. And their mysterious books, wrapped in brown shopping-bag paper, remained on the table next to the door, closed firmly behind them.

An accident of geography sent me to a school where all my classmates were white and many were the children of doctors and lawyers and business executives. On that first day of school, my classmates must certainly have been uneasy to find themselves apart from their families, in the first institution of their lives. But I was astonished. I was fated to be the "problem student" in class.

The nun said, in a friendly but oddly impersonal voice: "Boys and girls, this is Richard Rodriguez." (I heard her sound it out—*Rich-heard Road-ree-guess.*) It was the first time I had heard anyone say my name in English. "Richard," the nun repeated more slowly, writing my name down in her book. Quickly I turned to see my mother's face dissolve in a watery blur behind the pebbled-glass door.

Now, many years later, I hear of something called "bilingual education"—a scheme proposed in the late 1960s by Hispanic-American social activists, later endorsed by a congressional vote. It is a program that seeks to permit non-English-speaking children (many from lower-class homes) to use their "family language" as the language of school. Such, at least, is the aim its supporters announce. I hear them, and am forced to say no: It is not possible for a child, any child, ever to use his family's language in school. Not to understand this is to misunderstand the public uses of schooling and to trivialize the nature of intimate life.

Memory teaches me what I know of these matters. The boy reminds the adult. I was a bilingual child, but of a certain kind: "socially disadvantaged," the son of working-class parents, both Mexican immigrants.

---

[1] **Aria:** Italian for "air," usually refers to a song in an opera.

In the early years of my boyhood, my parents coped very well in America. My father had steady work. My mother managed at home. They were nobody's victims. When we moved to a house many blocks from the Mexican-American section of town, they were not intimidated by those two or three neighbors who initially tried to make us unwelcome. ("Keep your brats away from my sidewalk!") But despite all they achieved, or perhaps because they had so much to achieve, they lacked any deep feeling of ease, of belonging in public. They regarded the people at work or in crowds as being very distant from us. Those were the others, *los gringos*.[2] That term was interchangeable in their speech with another, even more telling: *los americanos*.

I grew up in a house where the only regular guests were my relations. On a certain day, enormous families of relatives would visit us, and there would be so many people that the noise and the bodies would spill out to the backyard and onto the front porch. Then for weeks no one would come. (If the doorbell rang, it was usually a salesman.) Our house stood apart—gaudy yellow in a row of white bungalows. We were the people with the noisy dog, the people who raised chickens. We were the foreigners on the block. A few neighbors would smile and wave at us. We waved back. But until I was seven years old, I did not know the name of the old couple living next door or the names of the kids living across the street.

In public, my father and mother spoke a hesitant, accented, and not always grammatical English. And then they would have to strain, their bodies tense, to catch the sense of what was rapidly said by *los gringos*. At home, they returned to Spanish. The language of their Mexican past sounded in counterpoint to the English spoken in public. The words would come quickly, with ease. Conveyed through those sounds was the pleasing, soothing, consoling reminder that one was at home.

During those years when I was first learning to speak, my mother and father addressed me only in Spanish; in Spanish I learned to reply. By contrast, English (*inglés*) was the language I came to associate with gringos, rarely heard in the house. I learned my first words of English overhearing my parents speaking to strangers. At six years of age, I knew just enough words for my mother to trust me on errands to stores one block away—but no more.

I was then a listening child, careful to hear the very different sounds of Spanish and English. Wide-eyed with hearing, I'd listen to sounds more than to words. First, there were English (gringo) sounds. So many words still were unknown to me that when the butcher or the lady at the drugstore said something, exotic polysyllabic sounds would bloom in the midst of their sentences. Often the speech of people in public seemed to me very loud, booming with confidence. The man behind the counter would literally ask, "What can I do for you?" But by being so firm and clear, the sound of his voice said that he was a gringo; he belonged in public society. There were also the high, nasal notes of middle-class American speech—which I

[2] *los gringos*: Spanish slang term for "the foreigners," usually Americans.

rarely am conscious of hearing today because I hear them so often, but could not stop hearing when I was a boy. Crowds at Safeway or at bus stops were noisy with the birdlike sounds of *los gringos.* I'd move away from them all—all the chirping chatter above me.

My own sounds I was unable to hear, but I knew that I spoke English poorly. My words could not extend to form complete thoughts. And the words I did speak I didn't know well enough to make distinct sounds. (Listeners would usually lower their heads to hear better what I was trying to say.) But it was one thing for *me* to speak English with difficulty; it was more troubling to hear my parents speaking in public: their high-whining vowels and guttural consonants; their sentences that got stuck with "eh" and "ah" sounds; the confused syntax; the hesitant rhythm of sounds so different from the way gringos spoke. I'd notice, moreover, that my parents' voices were softer than those of gringos we would meet.

I am tempted to say now that none of this mattered. (In adulthood I am embarrassed by childhood fears.) And, in a way, it didn't matter very much that my parents could not speak English with ease. Their linguistic difficulties had no serious consequences. My mother and father made themselves understood at the county hospital clinic and at government offices. And yet, in another way, it mattered very much. It was unsettling to hear my parents struggle with English. Hearing them, I'd grow nervous, and my clutching trust in their protection and power would be weakened.

There were many times like the night at a brightly lit gasoline station (a blaring white memory) when I stood uneasily hearing my father talk to a teenage attendant. I do not recall what they were saying, but I cannot forget the sounds my father made as he spoke. At one point his words slid together to form one long word—sounds as confused as the threads of blue and green oil in the puddle next to my shoes. His voice rushed through what he had left to say. Toward the end, he reached falsetto notes, appealing to his listener's understanding. I looked away at the lights of passing automobiles. I tried not to hear any more. But I heard only too well the attendant's reply, his calm, easy tones. Shortly afterward, headed for home, I shivered when my father put his hand on my shoulder. The very first chance that I got, I evaded his grasp and ran on ahead into the dark, skipping with feigned boyish exuberance.

But then there was Spanish: *español,* the language rarely heard away from the house; *español,* the language which seemed to me therefore a private language, my family's language. To hear its sounds was to feel myself specially recognized as one of the family, apart from *los otros.* A simple remark, an inconsequential comment could convey that assurance. My parents would say something to me and I would feel embraced by the sounds of their words. Those sounds said: *I am speaking with ease in Spanish. I am addressing you in words I never use with* los gringos. *I recognize you as someone special, close, like no one outside. You belong with us. In the family. Ricardo.*

At the age of six, well past the time when most middle-class children no longer notice the difference between sounds uttered at home and words spoken in public, I had a different experience. I lived in a world compounded of sounds. I was a child longer than most. I lived in a magical world, surrounded by sounds both pleasing and fearful. I shared with my family a language enchantingly private—different from that used in the city around us.

Just opening or closing the screen door behind me was an important experience. I'd rarely leave home all alone or without feeling reluctance. Walking down the sidewalk, under the canopy of tall trees, I'd warily notice the (suddenly) silent neighborhood kids who stood warily watching me. Nervously, I'd arrive at the grocery store to hear there the sounds of the gringo, reminding me that in this so-big world I was a foreigner. But if leaving home was never routine, neither was coming back. Walking toward our house, climbing the steps from the sidewalk, in summer when the front door was open, I'd hear voices beyond the screen door talking in Spanish. For a second or two I'd stay, linger there listening. Smiling, I'd hear my mother call out, saying in Spanish, "Is that you, Richard?" Those were her words, but all the while her sounds would assure me: *You are home now. Come closer inside. With us.* "*Sí*,"[3] I'd reply.

Once more inside the house, I would resume my place in the family. The sounds would grow harder to hear. Once more at home, I would grow less conscious of them. It required, however, no more than the blurt of the doorbell to alert me all over again to listen to sounds. The house would turn instantly quiet while my mother went to the door. I'd hear her hard English sounds. I'd wait to hear her voice turn to soft-sounding Spanish, which assured me, as surely as did the clicking tongue of the lock on the door, that the stranger was gone.

Plainly it is not healthy to hear such sounds so often. It is not healthy to distinguish public from private sounds so easily. I remained cloistered by sounds, timid and shy in public, too dependent on the voices at home. And yet I was a very happy child when I was at home. I remember many nights when my father would come back from work, and I'd hear him call out to my mother in Spanish, sounding relieved. In Spanish, his voice would sound the light and free notes that he never could manage in English. Some nights I'd jump up just hearing his voice. My brother and I would come running into the room where he was with our mother. Our laughing (so deep was the pleasure!) became screaming. Like others who feel the pain of public alienation, we transformed the knowledge of our public separateness into a consoling reminder of our intimacy. Excited, our voices joined in a celebration of sounds. *We are speaking now the way we never speak out in public—we are together,* the sounds told me. Some nights no one seemed willing to loosen the hold that sounds had on us. At dinner we invented new words that sounded Spanish, but made sense only to us. We pieced together new words by taking, say, an English verb and giving it Spanish endings. My mother's instructions at bedtime would be

---

[3] *Sí*: Spanish for "yes."

lacquered with mock-urgent tones. Or a word like *sí,* sounded in several notes, would convey added measures of feeling. Tongues lingered around the edges of words, especially fat vowels. And we happily sounded that military drum roll, the twirling roar of the Spanish *r.* Family language, my family's sounds: the voices of my parents and sisters and brother. Their voices insisting: *You belong here. We are family members. Related. Special to one another. Listen!* Voices singing and sighing, rising and straining, then surging, teeming with pleasure which burst syllables into fragments of laughter. At times it seemed there was steady quiet only when, from another room, the rustling whispers of my parents faded and I edged closer to sleep.

Supporters of bilingual education imply today that students like me miss a great deal by not being taught in their family's language. What they seem not to recognize is that, as a socially disadvantaged child, I regarded Spanish as a private language. It was a ghetto language that deepened and strengthened my feeling of public separateness. What I needed to learn in school was that I had the right, and the obligation, to speak the public language. The odd truth is that my first-grade classmates could have become bilingual, in the conventional sense of the word, more easily than I. Had they been taught early (as upper middle-class children often are taught) a "second language" like Spanish or French, they could have regarded it simply as another public language. In my case, such bilingualism could not have been so quickly achieved. What I did not believe was that I could speak a single public language.

Without question, it would have pleased me to have heard my teachers address me in Spanish when I entered the classroom. I would have felt much less afraid. I would have imagined that my instructors were somehow "related" to me; I would indeed have heard their Spanish as my family's language. I would have trusted them and responded with ease. But I would have delayed—postponed for how long?—having to learn the language of public society. I would have evaded—and for how long?—learning the great lesson of school: that I had a public identity.

Fortunately, my teachers were unsentimental about their responsibility. What they understood was that I needed to speak public English. So their voices would search me out, asking me questions. Each time I heard them I'd look up in surprise to see a nun's face frowning at me. I'd mumble, not really meaning to answer. The nun would persist. "Richard, stand up. Don't look at the floor. Speak up. Speak to the entire class, not just to me!" But I couldn't believe English could be my language to use. (In part, I did not want to believe it.) I continued to mumble. I resisted the teacher's demands. (Did I somehow suspect that once I learned this public language my family life would be changed?) Silent, waiting for the bell to sound, I remained dazed, diffident, afraid.

Because I wrongly imagined that English was intrinsically a public language and Spanish was intrinsically private, I easily noted the difference between classroom language and the language of home. At school, words were directed to a general audience of listeners. ("Boys and girls...") Words were meaningfully ordered. And the point was not self-expression alone, but to make oneself understood by many others. The teacher quizzed: "Boys and girls, why do we use that word in this sentence? Could we think of a better word to use there? Would the sentence change its meaning if the words were differently arranged? Isn't there a better way of saying much the same thing?" (I couldn't say. I wouldn't try to say.)

Three months passed. Five. A half year. Unsmiling, ever watchful, my teachers noted my silence. They began to connect my behavior with the slow progress my brother and sisters were making. Until, one Saturday morning, three nuns arrived at the house to talk to our parents. Stiffly they sat on the blue living-room sofa. From the doorway of another room, spying on the visitors, I noted the incongruity, the clash of two worlds, the faces and voices of school intruding upon the familiar setting of home. I overheard one voice gently wondering, "Do your children speak only Spanish at home, Mrs. Rodriguez?" While another voice added, "That Richard especially seems so timid and shy."

That Rich-heard!

With great tact, the visitors continued, "Is it possible for you and your husband to encourage your children to practice their English when they are home?" Of course my parents complied. What would they not do for their children's well-being? And how could they question the Church's authority which those women represented? In an instant they agreed to give up the language (the sounds) which had revealed and accentuated our family's closeness. The moment after the visitors left, the change was observed. "*Ahora,*[4] speak to us only *en inglés,*" my father and mother told us.

At first, it seemed a kind of game. After dinner each night, the family gathered together to practice "our" English. It was still then *inglés,* a language foreign to us, so we felt drawn to it as strangers. Laughing, we would try to define words we could not pronounce. We played with strange English sounds, often over-anglicizing our pronunciations. And we filled the smiling gaps of our sentences with familiar Spanish sounds. But that was cheating, somebody shouted, and everyone laughed.

In school, meanwhile, like my brother and sisters, I was required to attend a daily tutoring session. I needed a full year of this special work. I also needed my teachers to keep my attention from straying in class by calling out, "*Rich-heard!*"— their English voices slowly loosening the ties to my other name, with its three notes, *Ri-car-do.* Most of all, I needed to hear my mother and father speak to me in a moment of seriousness in "broken"—suddenly heartbreaking—English. This scene was inevitable. One Saturday morning I entered the kitchen where my parents were talking, but I did not realize that they were talking in Spanish until, the moment they saw me, their voices changed and they began speaking English. The gringo sounds they uttered startled me. Pushed me away. In that moment of trivial

---

[4] *Ahora:* Spanish for "now."

misunderstanding and profound insight, I felt my throat twisted by unsounded grief. I simply turned and left the room. But I had no place to escape to where I could grieve in Spanish. My brother and sisters were speaking English in another part of the house.

Again and again in the days following, as I grew increasingly angry, I was obliged to hear my mother and father encouraging me: "Speak to us *en inglés.*" Only then did I determine to learn classroom English. Thus, sometime afterward it happened: one day in school, I raised my hand to volunteer an answer to a question. I spoke out in a loud voice and I did not think it remarkable when the entire class understood. That day I moved very far from being the disadvantaged child I had been only days earlier. Taken hold at last was the belief, the calming assurance, that I *belonged* in public.

Shortly after, I stopped hearing the high, troubling sounds of *los gringos.* A more and more confident speaker of English, I didn't listen to how strangers sounded when they talked to me. With so many English-speaking people around me, I no longer heard American accents. Conversations quickened. Listening to persons whose voices sounded eccentrically pitched, I might note their sounds for a few seconds, but then I'd concentrate on what they were saying. Now when I heard someone's tone of voice—angry or questioning or sarcastic or happy or sad—I didn't distinguish it from the words it expressed. Sound and word were thus tightly wedded. At the end of each day I was often bemused, and always relieved, to realize how "soundless," though crowded with words, my day in public had been. An eight-year-old boy, I finally came to accept what had been technically true since my birth: I was an American citizen.

But diminished by then was the special feeling of closeness at home. Gone was the desperate, urgent, intense feeling of being at home among those with whom I felt intimate. Our family remained a loving family, but one greatly changed. We were no longer so close, no longer bound tightly together by the knowledge of our separateness from *los gringos.* Neither my older brother nor my sisters rushed home after school any more. Nor did I. When I arrived home, often there would be neighborhood kids in the house. Or the house would be empty of sounds.

Following the dramatic Americanization of their children, even my parents grew more publicly confident—especially my mother. First she learned the names of all the people on the block. Then she decided we needed to have a telephone in our house. My father, for his part, continued to use the word gringo, but it was no longer charged with bitterness or distrust. Stripped of any emotional content, the word simply became a name for those Americans not of Hispanic descent. Hearing him, sometimes, I wasn't sure if he was pronouncing the Spanish word *gringo,* or saying gringo in English.

There was a new silence at home. As we children learned more and more English, we shared fewer and fewer words with our parents. Sentences needed to be spoken slowly when one of us addressed our mother or father. Often the parent

wouldn't understand. The child would need to repeat himself. Still the parent mis-
understood. The young voice, frustrated, would end up saying, "Never mind"—the
subject was closed. Dinners would be noisy with the clinking of knives and forks
against dishes. My mother would smile softly between her remarks; my father, at the
other end of the table, would chew and chew his food while he stared over the heads
of his children.

My mother! My father! After English became my primary language, I no longer
knew what words to use in addressing my parents. The old Spanish words (those
tender accents of sound) I had earlier used—*mamá* and *papá*—I couldn't use any
more. They would have been all-too-painful reminders of how much had changed
in my life. On the other hand, the words I heard neighborhood kids call their parents seemed equally unsatisfactory. "Mother" and "father," "ma," "papa," "pa," "dad,"
"pop" (how I hated the all-American sound of that last word)—all these I felt were
unsuitable terms of address for *my* parents. As a result, I never used them at home.
Whenever I'd speak to my parents, I would try to get their attention by looking at
them. In public conversations, I'd refer to them as my "parents" or my "mother"
and "father."

My mother and father, for their part, responded differently, as their children
spoke to them less. My mother grew restless, seemed troubled and anxious at the
scarceness of words exchanged in the house. She would question me about my day
when I came home from school. She smiled at my small talk. She pried at the edges
of my sentences to get me to say something more. ("What…?") She'd join conversations she overheard, but her intrusions often stopped her children's talking. By contrast, my father seemed to grow reconciled to the new quiet. Though his English
somewhat improved, he tended more and more to retire into silence. At dinner he
spoke very little. One night his children and even his wife helplessly giggled at his
garbled English pronunciation of the Catholic "Grace Before Meals." Thereafter he
made his wife recite the prayer at the start of each meal, even on formal occasions
when there were guests in the house.

Hers became the public voice of the family. On official business it was she, not
my father, who would usually talk to strangers on the phone or in stores. We children grew so accustomed to his silence that years later we would routinely refer to
his "shyness." (My mother often tried to explain: both of his parents died when he
was eight. He was raised by an uncle who treated him as little more than a menial
servant. He was never encouraged to speak. He grew up alone—a man of few
words.) But I realized my father was not shy whenever I'd watch him speaking
Spanish with relatives. Using Spanish, he was quickly effusive. Especially when talking with other men, his voice would spark, flicker, flare alive with varied sounds. In
Spanish he expressed ideas and feelings he rarely revealed when speaking English.
With firm Spanish sounds he conveyed a confidence and authority that English
would never allow him.

The silence at home, however, was not simply the result of fewer words passing between parents and children. More profound for me was the silence created by my inattention to sounds. At about the time I no longer bothered to listen with care to the sounds of English in public, I grew careless about listening to the sounds made by the family when they spoke. Most of the time I would hear someone speaking at home and didn't distinguish his sounds from the words people uttered in public. I didn't even pay much attention to my parents' accented and ungrammatical speech—at least not at home. Only when I was with them in public would I become alert to their accents. But even then their sounds caused me less and less concern. For I was growing increasingly confident of my own public identity.

I would have been happier about my public success had I not recalled, sometimes, what it had been like earlier, when my family conveyed its intimacy through a set of conveniently private sounds. Sometimes in public, hearing a stranger, I'd hark back to my lost past. A Mexican farm worker approached me one day downtown. He wanted directions to some place. "*Hijito…,*" [5] he said. And his voice stirred old longings. Another time I was standing beside my mother in the visiting room of a Carmelite convent, before the dense screen which rendered the nuns shadowy figures. I heard several of them speaking Spanish in their busy, singsong, overlapping voices, assuring my mother that, yes, yes, we were remembered, all our family was remembered, in their prayers. Those voices echoed faraway family sounds. Another day a dark-faced old woman touched my shoulder lightly to steady herself as she boarded a bus. She murmured something to me I couldn't quite comprehend. Her Spanish voice came near, like the face of a never-before-seen relative in the instant before I was kissed. That voice, like so many of the Spanish voices I'd hear in public, recalled the golden age of my childhood.

Bilingual educators say today that children lose a degree of "individuality" by becoming assimilated into public society. (Bilingual schooling is a program popularized in the seventies, that decade when middle-class "ethnics" began to resist the process of assimilation—the "American melting pot.") But the bilingualists oversimplify when they scorn the value and necessity of assimilation. They do not seem to realize that a person is individualized in two ways. So they do not realize that, while one suffers a diminished sense of *private* individuality by being assimilated into public society, such assimilation makes possible the achievement of *public* individuality.

Simplistically again, the bilingualists insist that a student should be reminded of his difference from others in mass society, of his "heritage." But they equate mere separateness with individuality. The fact is that only in private—with intimates—is separateness from the crowd a prerequisite for individuality; an intimate "tells" me

[5] *Hijito*: Spanish for "sonny."

that I am unique, unlike all others, apart from the crowd. In public, by contrast, full individuality is achieved, paradoxically, by those who are able to consider themselves members of the crowd. Thus it happened for me. Only when I was able to think of myself as an American, no longer an alien in gringo society, could I seek the rights and opportunities necessary for full public individuality. The social and political advantages I enjoy as a man began on the day I came to believe that my name is indeed *Rich-heard Road-ree-guess*. It is true that my public society today is often impersonal; in fact, my public society is usually mass society. But despite the anonymity of the crowd, and despite the fact that the individuality I achieve in public is often tenuous—because it depends on my being one in a crowd—I celebrate the day I acquired my new name. Those middle-class ethnics who scorn assimilation seem to me filled with decadent self-pity, obsessed by the burden of public life. Dangerously, they romanticize public separateness and trivialize the dilemma of those who are truly socially disadvantaged.

If I rehearse here the changes in my private life after my Americanization, it is finally to emphasize a public gain. The loss implies the gain. The house I returned to each afternoon was quiet. Intimate sounds no longer greeted me at the door. Inside there were other noises. The telephone rang. Neighborhood kids ran past the door of the bedroom where I was reading my schoolbooks—covered with brown shopping-bag paper. Once I learned the public language, it would never again be easy for me to hear intimate family voices. More and more of my day was spent hearing words, not sounds. But that may only be a way of saying that on the day I raised my hand in class and spoke loudly to an entire roomful of faces, my childhood started to end.

—1981

Ana Menéndez (b. 1970)

As the daughter of Cubans who left their homeland with the idea of returning to the island-nation "very soon," Ana Menéndez dramatizes, with intense expressive detail, the experience of exiles anywhere, anytime. Her characters struggle to find a sense of belonging while maintaining their cultural identity through food, games, music, and language. Her work points to the obsession of Cuban immigrants with idealized memories ("In Cuba I remember … life was good and pure") that prevents them from acknowledging that their utopia disintegrated long ago. She also shows how nostalgia is an obstacle to putting down roots in America ("Here in America, I may be a short, insignificant mutt, but in Cuba I was a German Shepherd."). She blends heartbreaking laughter with Chekhovian compassion and a Proustian evocation of the past.

Menéndez was born in Los Angeles, California, but most of her fiction takes place physically and mentally between Cuba and Miami. She studied journalism at Florida International University and received her Masters in writing from New York University. She worked as a reporter for the *Orange County Register* in California, and is now an Opinion columnist for the *Miami Herald*. She finds her inspiration in poetry and the classics. Writers who have influenced her work include José Martí, Guillermo Cabrera Infante, Reinaldo Arenas, and Beat poets.

Ana Menéndez won a Pushcart Prize for her collection of short stories *In Cuba I Was a German Shepherd* (2001). She has also published a novel, *Loving Che* (2003).

Further Reading   Robert Birnbaum, "Personalities: Birnbaum v. Ana Menéndez," <http://www.themorningnews.org> (2004); Lene Johannessen, "The Lonely Figure: Memory of Exile in Ana Menéndez's 'In Cuba I Was a German Shepherd,'" *Journal of Postcolonial Writing*, 41.1, pp. 54–68; Maya Socolovsky, "Cuba Interrupted: The Loss of Center and Story in Ana Menéndez," *Critique: Studies in Contemporary Fiction* <http://findarticles.com> (Spring 2005).

—*Rei Berroa, George Mason University*

For many Cuban immigrants, such as those in Menéndez's story, the reign of Fidel Castro has caused enormous grief and anger. To escape Cuba, refugees have tried to cross the ocean to Florida in all sorts of crafts, often dying in the process.

AP Photo/Lynne Sladky

In Cuba I Was a German Shepherd

The park where the four men gathered was small. Before the city put it on its tourist maps, it was just a fenced rectangle of space that people missed on the way to their office jobs. The men came each morning to sit under the shifting shade of a banyan tree, and sometimes the way the wind moved through the leaves reminded them of home.

One man carried a box of plastic dominos. His name was Máximo, and because he was a small man his grandiose name had inspired much amusement all his life. He liked to say that over the years he'd learned a thing or two about the physics of laughter and his friends took that to mean good humor could make a big man out of anyone. Now Máximo waited for the others to sit before turning the dominos out on the table. Judging the men to be in good spirits, he cleared his throat and began to tell the joke he had prepared for the day.

"So Bill Clinton dies in office and they freeze his body."

Antonio leaned back in his chair and let out a sigh. "Here we go."

Máximo caught a roll of the eyes and almost grew annoyed. But he smiled. "It gets better."

He scraped the dominos in two wide circles across the table, then continued.

"Okay, so they freeze his body and when we get the technology to unfreeze him, he wakes up in the year 2105."

"Two thousand one hundred and five, eh?"

"Very good," Máximo said. "Anyway, he's curious about what's happened to the world all this time, so he goes up to a Jewish fellow and he says, 'So, how are things in the Middle East?' The guy replies, 'Oh wonderful, wonderful, everything is like heaven. Everybody gets along now.' This makes Clinton smile, right?"

The men stopped shuffling and dragged their pieces across the table and waited for Máximo to finish.

"Next he goes up to an Irishman and he says, 'So how are things over there in Northern Ireland now?' The guy says, 'Northern? It's one Ireland now and we all live in peace.' Clinton is extremely pleased at this point, right? So he does that biting thing with his lip."

Máximo stopped to demonstrate and Raúl and Carlos slapped their hands on the domino table and laughed. Máximo paused. Even Antonio had to smile. Máximo loved this moment when the men were warming to the joke and he still kept the punch line close to himself like a secret.

"So, okay," Máximo continued, "Clinton goes up to a Cuban fellow and says, 'Compadre,[1] how are things in Cuba these days?' The guy looks at Clinton and he

---

[1] **Compadre:** Spanish for "friend."

says to the president, 'Let me tell you, my friend, I can feel it in my bones: Any day now Castro's[2] gonna fall.'"

Máximo tucked his head into his neck and smiled. Carlos slapped him on the back and laughed.

"That's a good one, sure is," he said. "I like that one."

"Funny," Antonio said, nodding as he set up his pieces.

"Yes, funny," Raúl said. After chuckling for another moment, he added, "But old."

"What do you mean old?" Antonio said, then he turned to Carlos. "What are you looking at?"

Carlos stopped laughing.

"It's not old," Máximo said. "I just made it up."

"I'm telling you, professor, it's an old one," Raúl said. "I heard it when Reagan[3] was president."

Máximo looked at Raúl, but didn't say anything. He pulled the double nine from his row and laid it in the middle of the table, but the thud he intended was lost in the horns and curses of morning traffic on Eighth Street.

* * *

Raúl and Máximo had lived on the same El Vedado street in Havana for fifteen years before the revolution. Raúl had been a government accountant and Máximo a professor at the University, two blocks from his home on L Street. They weren't close friends, but friendly still in that way of people who come from the same place and think they already know the important things about one another.

Máximo was one of the first to leave L Street, boarding a plane for Miami on the eve of the first of January 1961, exactly two years after Batista had done the same. For reasons he told himself he could no longer remember, he said good-bye to no one. He was thirty-six years old then, already balding, with a wife and two young daughters whose names he tended to confuse. He left behind the row house of long shiny windows, the piano, the mahogany furniture, and the pension he thought he'd return to in two years' time. Three if things were as serious as they said.

In Miami, Máximo tried driving a taxi, but the streets were a web of foreign names and winding curves that could one day lead to glitter and another to the hollow end of a pistol. His Spanish and his University of Havana credentials meant nothing here. And he was too old to cut sugarcane with the younger men who began arriving in the spring of 1961. But the men gave Máximo an idea, and after teary nights of

---

[2] **Fidel Castro** (b. 1926): Former president of Cuba; he took charge after leading a revolution against Cuba's authoritarian leader Batista in 1959.

[3] **Ronald Reagan** (1911–2004): U.S. President from 1981 to 1989.

promises, he convinced his wife—she of stately homes and multiple cooks—to make lunch to sell to those sugar men who waited, squatting on their heels in the dark, for the bus to Belle Glade every morning. They worked side by side, Máximo and Rosa. And at the end of every day, their hands stained orange from the lard and the cheap meat, their knuckles red and tender where the hot water and the knife blade had worked their business, Máximo and Rosa would sit down to whatever remained of the day's cooking and they would chew slowly, the day unraveling, their hunger ebbing away with the light.

They worked together for years like that, and when the Cubans began disappearing from the bus line, Máximo and Rosa moved their lunch packets indoors and opened their little restaurant right on Eighth Street. There, a generation of former professors served black beans and rice to the nostalgic. When Raúl showed up in Miami one summer looking for work, Máximo added one more waiter's spot for his old acquaintance from L Street. Each night, after the customers had gone, Máximo and Rosa and Raúl and Havana's old lawyers and bankers and dreamers would sit around the biggest table and eat and talk and sometimes, late in the night after several glasses of wine, someone would start the stories that began with "In Cuba I remember." They were stories of old lovers, beautiful and round-hipped. Of skies that stretched on clear and blue to the Cuban hills. Of green landscapes that clung to the red clay of Güines, roots dug in like fingernails in a good-bye. In Cuba, the stories always began, life was good and pure. But something always happened to them in the end, something withering, malignant. Máximo never understood it. The stories that opened in sun, always narrowed into a dark place. And after those nights, his head throbbing, Máximo would turn and turn in his sleep and awake unable to remember his dreams.

Even now, five years after selling the place, Máximo couldn't walk by it in the early morning when it was still clean and empty. He'd tried it once. He'd stood and stared into the restaurant and had become lost and dizzy in his own reflection in the glass, the neat row of chairs, the tombstone lunch board behind them.

* * *

"Okay. A bunch of rafters are on the beach getting ready to sail off to Miami."

"Where are they?"

"Who cares? Wherever. Cuba's got a thousand miles of coastline. Use your imagination."

"Let the professor tell his thing, for God's sake."

"Thank you." Máximo cleared his throat and shuffled the dominos. "So anyway, a bunch of rafters are gathered there on the sand. And they're all crying and hugging their wives and all the rafts are bobbing on the water and suddenly someone in the group yells, 'Hey! Look who goes there!' And it's Fidel in swimming trunks, carrying a raft on his back."

Carlos interrupted to let out a yelping laugh. "I like that, I like it, sure do."

"You like it, eh?" said Antonio. "Why don't you let the Cuban finish it?"

Máximo slid the pieces to himself in twos and continued. "So one of the guys on the sand says to Fidel, 'Compatriota, what are you doing here? What's with the raft?' And Fidel sits on his raft and pushes off the shore and says, 'I'm sick of this place too. I'm going to Miami.' So the other guys look at each other and say, 'Coño, compadre, if you're leaving, then there's no reason for us to go. Here, take my raft too, and get the fuck out of here.'"

Raúl let a shaking laugh rise from his belly and saluted Máximo with a domino piece.

"A good one, my friend."

Carlos laughed long and loud. Antonio laughed too, but he was careful not to laugh too hard and he gave his friend a sharp look over the racket he was causing. He and Carlos were Dominican, not Cuban, and they ate their same foods and played their same games, but Antonio knew they still didn't understand all the layers of hurt in the Cubans' jokes.

* * *

It had been Raúl's idea to go down to Domino Park that first time. Máximo protested. He had seen the rows of tourists pressed up against the fence, gawking at the colorful old guys playing dominos.

"I'm not going to be the sad spectacle in someone's vacation slide show," he'd said.

But Raúl was already dressed up in a pale blue guayabera, saying how it was a beautiful day and smell the air.

"Let them take pictures," Raúl said. "What the hell. Make us immortal."

"Immortal," Máximo said like a sneer. And then to himself, The gods' punishment.

It was that year after Rosa died and Máximo didn't want to tell how he'd begun to see her at the kitchen table as she'd been at twenty-five. Watched one thick strand of her dark hair stuck to her morning face. He saw her at thirty, bending down to wipe the chocolate off the cheeks of their two small daughters. And his eyes moved from Rosa to his small daughters. He had something he needed to tell them. He saw them grown up, at the funeral, crying together. He watched Rosa rise and do the sign of the cross. He knew he was caught inside a nightmare, but he couldn't stop. He would emerge slowly, creaking out of the shower and there she'd be, Rosa, like before, her breasts round and pink from the hot water, calling back through the years. Some mornings he would awake and smell peanuts roasting and hear the faint call of the manicero pleading for someone to relieve his burden of white paper cones. Or it would be thundering, the long hard thunder of Miami that was so much like the thunder of home that each rumble shattered the morning of his other life. He would awake, caught fast in the damp sheets, and feel himself falling backwards.

He took the number eight bus to Eighth Street and 15th Avenue. At Domino Park, he sat with Raúl and they played alone that first day, Máximo noticing his own speckled hands, the spots of light through the banyan leaves, a round red beetle that crawled slowly across the table, then hopped the next breeze and floated away.

* * *

Antonio and Carlos were not Cuban, but they knew when to dump their heavy pieces and when to hold back the eights for the final shocking stroke. Waiting for a table, Raúl and Máximo would linger beside them and watch them lay their traps, a succession of threes that broke their opponents, an incredible run of fives. Even the unthinkable: passing when they had the piece to play.

Other twosomes began to refuse to play with the Dominicans, said that tipo Carlos gave them the creeps with his giggling and monosyllables. Besides, any team that won so often must be cheating, went the charge, especially a team one-half imbecile. But really it was that no one plays to lose. You begin to lose again and again and it reminds you of other things in your life, the despair of it all begins to bleed through and that is not what games are for. Who wants to live their whole life alongside the lucky? But Máximo and Raúl liked these blessed Dominicans, appreciated the well-oiled moves of two old pros. And if the two Dominicans, afraid to be alone again, let them win now and then, who would know, who could ever admit to such a thing?

For many months they didn't know much about each other, these four men. Even the smallest boy knew not to talk when the pieces were in play. But soon came Máximo's jokes during the shuffling, something new and bright coming into his eyes like daydreams as he spoke. Carlos' full loud laughter, like that of children. And the four men learned to linger long enough between sets to color an old memory while the white pieces scraped along the table.

One day as they sat at their table closest to the sidewalk, a pretty girl walked by. She swung her long brown hair around and looked in at the men with her green eyes.

"What the hell is she looking at?" said Antonio, who always sat with his back to the wall, looking out at the street. But the others saw how he returned the stare too.

Carlos let out a giggle and immediately put a hand to his mouth.

"In Santo Domingo,[4] a man once looked at—" But Carlos didn't get to finish.

"Shut up, you old idiot," said Antonio, putting his hands on the table like he was about to get up and leave.

----

[4] **Santo Domingo:** Capital city of the Dominican Republic, an island east of Cuba.

"Please," Máximo said.

The girl stared another moment, then turned and left. Raúl rose slowly, flattening down his oiled hair with his right hand.

"Ay, mi niña."[5]

"Sit down, hombre,"[6] Antonio said. "You're an old fool, just like this one."

"You're the fool," Raúl called back. "A woman like that…" He watched the girl cross the street. When she was out of sight, he grabbed the back of the chair behind him and eased his body down, his eyes still on the street. The other three men looked at one another.

"I knew a woman like that once," Raúl said after a long moment.

"That's right, he did," Antonio said, "in his moist boy dreams—what was it? A century ago?"

"No me jodas,"[7] Raúl said. "You are a vulgar man. I had a life all three of you would have paid millions for. Women."

Máximo watched him, then lowered his face, shuffled the dominos.

"I had women," Raúl said.

"We all had women," Carlos said, and he looked like he was about to laugh again, but instead just sat there, smiling like he was remembering one of Máximo's jokes.

"There was one I remember. More beautiful than the rising moon," Raúl said.

"Oh Jesus," Antonio said. "You people."

Máximo looked up, watching Raúl.

"Ay, a woman like that," Raúl said and shook his head. "The women of Cuba were radiant, magnificent, wouldn't you say, professor?"

Máximo looked away.

"I don't know," Antonio said. "I think that Americana there looked better than anything you remember."

And that brought a long laugh from Carlos.

Máximo sat all night at the pine table in his new efficiency, thinking about the green-eyed girl and wondering why he was thinking about her. The table and a narrow bed had come with the apartment, which he'd moved into after selling their house in Shenandoah. The table had come with two chairs, sturdy and polished—not in the least institutional—but he had moved the other chair by the bed.

The landlady, a woman in her forties, had helped Máximo haul up three potted palms. Later, he bought a green pot of marigolds he saw in the supermarket and brought its butter leaves back to life under the window's eastern light. Máximo often sat at the table through the night, sometimes reading Martí, sometimes listening to the rain on the tin hull of the air conditioner.

---

[5] "Ay, mi niña": Spanish for "Ah, my child."
[6] hombre: Spanish for "man."
[7] "No me jodas": Spanish slang for "Don't screw around with me."

When you are older, he'd read somewhere, you don't need as much sleep. And wasn't that funny because his days felt more like sleep than ever. Dinner kept him occupied for hours, remembering the story of each dish. Sometimes, at the table, he greeted old friends and awakened with a start when they reached out to touch him. When dawn rose and slunk into the room sideways through the blinds, Máximo walked as in a dream across the thin patterns of light on the terrazzo. The chair, why did he keep the other chair? Even the marigolds reminded him. An image returned again and again. Was it the green-eyed girl?

And then he remembered that Rosa wore carnations in her hair and hated her name. And that it saddened him because he liked to roll it off his tongue like a slow train to the country.

"Rosa," he said, taking her hand the night they met at La Concha while an old danzón[8] played.

"Clavel," she said, tossing her head back in a crackling laugh. "Call me Clavel."

She pulled her hand away and laughed again. "Don't you notice the flower in a girl's hair?"

He led her around the dance floor, lined with chaperones, and when they turned he whispered that he wanted to follow her laughter to the moon. She laughed again, the notes round and heavy as summer raindrops, and Máximo felt his fingers go cold where they touched hers. The danzón played and they turned and turned and the faces of the chaperones and the moist warm air—and Máximo with his cold fingers worried that she had laughed at him. He was twenty-four and could not imagine a more sorrowful thing in all the world.

Sometimes, years later, he would catch a premonition of Rosa in the face of his eldest daughter. She would turn toward a window or do something with her eyes. And then she would smile and tilt her head back and her laughter connected him again to that night, made him believe for a moment his life was a string you could gather up in your hands all at once.

He sat at the table and tried to remember the last time he saw Marisa. In California now. An important lawyer. A year? Two? Anabel, gone to New York? Two years? They called more often than most children, Máximo knew. They called often and he was lucky that way.

* * *

"Fidel decides he needs to get in touch with young people."

"Ay, ay, ay."

"So his handlers arrange for him to go to a school in Havana. He gets all dressed up in his olive uniform, you know, puts conditioner on his beard and brushes it one hundred times, all that."

---

[8] *danzón*: Spanish for "Cuban dance music."

Raúl breathed out, letting each breath come out like a puff of laughter. "Where do you get these things?"

"No interrupting the artist anymore, okay?" Máximo continued. "So after he's beautiful enough, he goes to the school. He sits in on a few classes, walks around the halls. Finally, it's time for Fidel to leave and he realizes he hasn't talked to anyone. He rushes over to the assembly that is seeing him off with shouts of 'Comandante!' and he pulls a little boy out of a row. 'Tell me,' Fidel says, 'what is your name?' 'Pepito,' the little boy answers. 'Pepito—what a nice name,' Fidel says. 'And tell me, Pepito, what do you think of the revolution?' 'Comandante,' Pepito says, 'the revolution is the reason we are all here.' 'Ah, very good, Pepito. And tell me, what is your favorite subject?' Pepito answers, 'Comandante, my favorite subject is mathematics.' Fidel pats the little boy on the head. 'And tell me, Pepito, what would you like to be when you grow up?' Pepito smiles and says, 'Comandante, I would like to be a tourist.'"

Máximo looked around the table, a shadow of a smile on his thin white lips as he waited for the laughter.

"Ay," Raúl said. "That is so funny it breaks my heart."

* * *

Máximo grew to like dominos, the way each piece became part of the next. After the last piece was laid down and they were tallying up the score, Máximo liked to look over the table as an artist might. He liked the way the row of black dots snaked around the table with such free-flowing abandon it was almost as if, thrilled to be let out of the box, the pieces choreographed a fresh dance of gratitude every night. He liked the straight forward contrast of black on white. The clean, fresh scrape of the pieces across the table before each new round. The audacity of the double nines. The plain smooth face of the blank, like a newborn unetched by the world to come.

"Professor," Raúl began. "Let's speed up the shuffling a bit, sí?"

"I was thinking," Máximo said.

"Well, that shouldn't take long," Antonio said.

"Who invented dominos, anyway?" Máximo said.

"I'd say it was probably the Chinese," Antonio said.

"No jodas," Raúl said. "Who else could have invented this game of skill and intelligence but a Cuban?"

"Coño,"[9] said Antonio without a smile. "Here we go again."

"Ah, bueno,"[10] Raúl said with a smile stuck between joking and condescending. "You don't have to believe it if it hurts."

Carlos let out a long laugh.

---

[9] *Coño*: Spanish for "damn it."
[10] *"Ah, bueno"*: Spanish for "Oh, good."

"You people are unbelievable," said Antonio. But there was something hard and tired behind the way he smiled.

* * *

It was the first day of December, but summer still hung about in the brightest patches of sunlight. The four men sat under the shade of the banyan tree. It wasn't cold, not even in the shade, but three of the men wore cardigans. If asked, they would say they were expecting a chilly north wind and doesn't anybody listen to the weather forecasts anymore. Only Antonio, his round body enough to keep him warm, clung to the short sleeves of summer.

Kids from the local Catholic high school had volunteered to decorate the park for Christmas and they dashed about with tinsel in their hair, bumping one another and laughing loudly. Lucinda, the woman who issued the dominos and kept back the gambling, asked them to quiet down, pointing at the men. A wind stirred the top branches of the banyan tree and moved on without touching the ground. One leaf fell to the table.

Antonio waited for Máximo to fetch Lucinda's box of plastic pieces. Antonio held his brown paper bag to his chest and looked at the Cubans, his customary sourness replaced for a moment by what in a man like him could pass for levity. Máximo sat down and began to dump the plastic pieces on the table as he always did. But this time, Antonio held out his hand.

"One moment," he said and shook his brown paper bag.

"¿Qué pasa, chico?"[11] Máximo said.

Antonio reached into the paper bag as the men watched. He let the paper fall away. In his hand he held an oblong black leather box.

"Coñooo," Raúl said.

Antonio set the box on the table, like a magician drawing out his trick. He looked around to the men and finally opened the box with a flourish to reveal a neat row of big heavy pieces, gone yellow and smooth like old teeth. They bent in closer to look. Antonio tilted the box gently and the pieces fell out in one long line, their black dots facing up now like tight dark pupils in the sunlight.

"Ivory," Antonio said. "And ebony. It's an antique. You're not allowed to make them anymore."

"Beautiful," Carlos said and clasped his hands.

"My daughter found them for me in New Orleans," Antonio continued, ignoring Carlos.

He looked around the table and lingered on Máximo, who had lowered the box of plastic dominos to the ground.

---

[11] "*¿Qué pasa, chico?*": Spanish for "How's it going, boy?"

"She said she's been searching for them for two years. Couldn't wait two more weeks to give them to me," he said.

"Coñooo," Raúl said.

A moment passed.

"Well," Antonio said, "what do you think, Máximo?"

Máximo looked at him. Then he bent across the table to touch one of the pieces. He gave a jerk with his head and listened for the traffic. "Very nice," he said.

"Very nice?" Antonio said. "Very nice?" He laughed in his thin way. "My daughter walked all over New Orleans to find this and the Cuban thinks it's 'very nice'?" He paused, watching Máximo. "Did you know my daughter is coming to visit me for Christmas, Máximo? Maybe you can tell her that her gift was very nice, but not as nice as some you remember, eh?"

Máximo looked up, his eyes settling on Carlos, who looked at Antonio and then looked away.

"Calm down, hombre," Carlos said, opening his arms wide, a nervous giggle beginning in his throat. "What's gotten into you?"

Antonio waved his hand and sat down. A diesel truck rattled down Eighth Street, headed for downtown.

"My daughter is a district attorney in Los Angeles," Máximo said after the noise of the truck died. "December is one of the busiest months."

He felt a heat behind his eyes he had not felt in many years.

"Feel one in your hand," Antonio said. "Feel how heavy that is."

* * *

When the children were small, Máximo and Rosa used to spend Nochebuena with his cousins in Cárdenas. It was a five-hour drive from Havana in the cars of those days. They would rise early on the twenty-third and arrive by mid-afternoon so Máximo could help the men kill the pig for the feast the following night. Máximo and the other men held the squealing, squirming animal down, its wiry brown coat cutting into their gloveless hands. But God, they were intelligent creatures. No sooner did it spot the knife than the animal bolted out of their arms, screaming like Armageddon. It had become the subtext to the Nochebuena[12] tradition, this chasing of the terrified pig through the yard, dodging orange trees and rotting fruit underneath. The children were never allowed to watch, Rosa made sure. They sat indoors with the women and stirred the black beans. With loud laughter, they shut out the shouts of the men and the hysterical pleadings of the animal as it was dragged back to its slaughter.

---

[12] *Nochebuena:* Spanish for "Christmas Eve."

* * *

"Juanito the little dog gets off the boat from Cuba and decides to take a little stroll down Brickell Avenue."

"Let me make sure I understand the joke. Juanito is a dog. Bowwow."

"That's pretty good."

"Yes, Juanito is a dog, goddamn it."

Raúl looked up, startled.

Máximo shuffled the pieces hard and swallowed. He swung his arms across the table in wide, violent arcs. One of the pieces flew off the table.

"Hey, hey, watch it with that, what's wrong with you?"

Máximo stopped. He felt his heart beating. "I'm sorry," he said. He bent over the edge of the table to see where the piece had landed. "Wait a minute." He held the table with one hand and tried to stretch to pick up the piece.

"What are you doing?"

"Just wait a minute." When he couldn't reach, he stood, pulled the piece toward him with his foot, sat back down, and reached for it again, this time grasping it between his fingers and his palm. He put it facedown on the table with the others and shuffled, slowly, his mind barely registering the traffic.

"Where was I—Juanito the little dog, right, bowwow." Máximo took a deep breath. "He's just off the boat from Cuba and is strolling down Brickell Avenue. He's looking up at all the tall and shiny buildings. 'Coñoo,' he says, dazzled by all the mirrors. 'There's nothing like this in Cuba.'"

"Hey, hey, professor. We had tall buildings."

"Jesus Christ!" Máximo said. He pressed his thumb and forefinger into the corners of his eyes. "This is after Castro, then. Let me just get it out for Christ's sake."

He stopped shuffling. Raúl looked away.

"Ready now? Juanito the little dog is looking up at all the tall buildings and he's so happy to finally be in America because all his cousins have been telling him what a great country it is, right? You know, they were sending back photos of their new cars and girlfriends."

"A joke about dogs who drive cars—I've heard it all."

"Hey, they're Cuban super-dogs."

"All right, they're sending back photos of their new owners or the biggest bones any dog has ever seen. Anything you like. Use your imaginations." Máximo stopped shuffling. "Where was I?"

"You were at the part where Juanito buys a Rolls-Royce."[13]

The men laughed.

---

[13] **Rolls-Royce:** Brand name of a luxury car.

"Okay, Antonio, why don't you three fools continue the joke." Máximo got up from the table. "You've made me forget the rest of it."

"Aw, come on, chico, sit down, don't be so sensitive."

"Come on, professor, you were at the part where Juanito is so glad to be in America."

"Forget it. I can't remember the rest now."

Máximo rubbed his temple, grabbed the back of the chair, and sat down slowly, facing the street. "Just leave me alone, I can't remember it." He pulled at the pieces two by two. "I'm sorry. Look, let's just play."

The men set up their double rows of dominos, like miniature barricades before them.

"These pieces are a work of art," Antonio said and laid down a double eight.

The banyan tree was strung with white lights that were lit all day. Colored lights twined around the metal poles of the fence, which was topped with a long loping piece of gold tinsel garland.

The Christmas tourists began arriving just before lunch as Máximo and Raúl stepped off the number eight. Carlos and Antonio were already at the table, watched by two groups of families. Mom and Dad with kids. They were big; even the kids were big and pink. The mother whispered to the kids and they smiled and waved. Raúl waved back at the mother.

"Nice legs, yes," he whispered to Máximo.

Before Máximo looked away, he saw the mother take out a little black pocket camera. He saw the flash out of the corner of his eye. He sat down and looked around the table; the other men stared at their pieces.

The game started badly. It happened sometimes—the distribution of the pieces went all wrong and out of desperation one of the men made mistakes and soon it was all they could do not to knock all the pieces over and start fresh. Raúl set down a double three and signaled to Máximo it was all he had. Carlos passed. Máximo surveyed his last five pieces. His thoughts scattered to the family outside. He looked to find the tallest boy with his face pressed between the iron slats, staring at him.

"You pass?" Antonio said.

Máximo looked at him, then at the table. He put down a three and a five. He looked again; the boy was gone. The family had moved on.

The tour groups arrived later that afternoon. First the white buses with the happy blue letters WELCOME TO LITTLE HAVANA. Next, the fat women in white shorts, their knees lost in an abstraction of flesh. Máximo tried to concentrate on the game. The worst part was how the other men acted out for them. Dominos are supposed to be a quiet game. And now there they were shouting at each other and gesturing. A few of the men had even brought cigars, and they dangled now, unlit, from their mouths.

"You see, Raúl," Máximo said. "You see how we're a spectacle?" He felt like an animal and wanted to growl and cast about behind the metal fence.

Raúl shrugged. "Doesn't bother me."

"A goddamn spectacle. A collection of old bones," Máximo said.

The other men looked up at Máximo.

"Hey, speak for yourself, cabron," Antonio said.

Raúl shrugged again.

Máximo rubbed his knuckles and began to shuffle the pieces. It was hot, and the sun was setting in his eyes, back-lighting the car exhaust like a veil before him. He rubbed his temple, feeling the skin move over the bone. He pressed the inside corners of his eyes, then drew his hand back over the pieces.

"Hey, you okay there?" Antonio said.

An open trolley pulled up and parked on the curb. A young man with blond hair, perhaps in his thirties, stood up in the front, holding a microphone. He wore a guayabera. Máximo looked away.

"This here is Domino Park," came the amplified voice in English, then Spanish. "No one under fifty-five allowed, folks. But we can sure watch them play."

Máximo heard shutters click, then convinced himself he couldn't have heard, not from where he was.

"Most of these men are Cuban and they're keeping alive the tradition of their homeland," the amplified voice continued, echoing against the back wall of the park. "You see, in Cuba, it was very common to retire to a game of dominos after a good meal. It was a way to bond and build community. Folks, you here are seeing a slice of the past. A simpler time of good friendships and unhurried days."

Maybe it was the sun. The men later noted that he seemed odd. The tics. Rubbing his bones.

First Máximo muttered to himself. He shuffled automatically. When the feedback on the microphone pierced through Domino Park, he could no longer sit where he was, accept things as they were. It was a moment that had long been missing from his life.

He stood and made a fist at the trolley.

"Mierda!"[14] he shouted. "Mierda! That's the biggest bullshit I've ever heard."

He made a lunge at the fence. Carlos jumped up and restrained him. Raúl led him back to his seat.

The man of the amplified voice cleared his throat. The people on the trolley looked at him and back at Máximo; perhaps they thought this was part of the show.

"Well." The man chuckled. "There you have it, folks."

---

[14] *"Mierda!"*: Spanish for "shit."

Lucinda ran over, but the other men waved her off. She began to protest about rules and propriety. The park had a reputation to uphold.

It was Antonio who spoke.

"Leave the man alone," he said.

Máximo looked at him. His head was pounding. Antonio met his gaze briefly, then looked to Lucinda.

"Some men don't like to be stared at is all," he said. "It won't happen again."

She shifted her weight, but remained where she was, watching.

"What are you waiting for?" Antonio said, turning now to Máximo, who had lowered his head into the white backs of the dominos. "Let's play."

That night Máximo was too tired to sit at the pine table. He didn't even prepare dinner. He slept, and in his dreams he was a green and yellow fish swimming in warm waters, gliding through the coral, the only fish in the sea and he was happy. But the light changed and the sea darkened suddenly and he was rising through it, afraid of breaking the surface, afraid of the pinhole sun on the other side, afraid of drowning in the blue vault of sky.

*   *   *

"Let me finish the story of Juanito the little dog."

No one said anything.

"Is that okay? I'm okay. I just remembered it. Can I finish it?"

The men nodded, but still did not speak.

"He is just off the boat from Cuba. He is walking down Brickell Avenue. And he is trying to steady himself, see, because he still has his sea legs and all the buildings are so tall they are making him dizzy. He doesn't know what to expect. He's maybe a little afraid. And he's thinking about a pretty little dog he knew once and he's wondering where she is now and he wishes he were back home."

He paused to take a breath. Raúl cleared his throat. The men looked at one another, then at Máximo. But his eyes were on the blur of dominos before him. He felt a stillness around him, a shadow move past the fence, but he didn't look up.

"He's not a depressive kind of dog, though. Don't get me wrong. He's very feisty. And when he sees an elegant white poodle striding toward him, he forgets all his worries and exclaims, 'O Madre de Dios, si cocinas como cominas…'"[15]

The men let out a small laugh. Máximo continued.

"'Si cocinas como caminas…,' Junito says, but the white poodle interrupts and says, 'I beg your pardon? This is America—kindly speak English.' So Juanito pauses for a moment to consider and says in his broken English, 'Mamita, you are one hot doggie, yes? I would like to take you to movies and fancy dinners.'"

[15] *"O Madre de Dios, si cocinas como caminas …"*: "Oh mother of God, she walks like a kitchen."

"One hot doggie, yes?" Carlos repeated, then laughed. "You're killing me." The other men smiled, warming to the story as before.

"So Juanito says, 'I would like to marry you, my love, and have gorgeous puppies with you and live in a castle.' Well, all this time the white poodle has her snout in the air. She looks at Juanito and says, 'Do you have any idea who you're talking to? I am a refined breed of considerable class and you are nothing but a short, insignificant mutt.' Juanito is stunned for a moment, but he rallies for the final shot. He's a proud dog, you see, and he's afraid of his pain. 'Pardon me, your highness,' Juanito the mangy dog says. 'Here in America, I may be a short, insignificant mutt, but in Cuba I was a German shepherd.'"

Máximo turned so the men would not see his tears. The afternoon traffic crawled eastward. One horn blasted, then another. He remembered holding his daughters days after their birth, thinking how fragile and vulnerable lay his bond to the future. For weeks, he carried them on pillows, like jeweled china. Then the blank spaces in his life lay before him. Now he stood with the gulf at his back, their ribbony youth aflutter in the past. And what had he salvaged from the years? Already, he was forgetting Rosa's face, the precise shade of her eyes.

Carlos cleared his throat and moved his hand as if to touch him, then held back. He cleared his throat again.

"He was a good dog," Carlos said and pressed his lips together.

Antonio began to laugh, then fell silent with the rest. Máximo started shuffling, then stopped. The shadow of the banyan tree worked a kaleidoscope over the dominos. When the wind eased, Máximo tilted his head to listen. He heard something stir behind him, someone leaning heavily on the fence. He could almost feel the breath. His heart quickened.

"Tell them to go away," Máximo said. "Tell them, no pictures."

—2001

Credits